JEW FACE

A STORY OF LOVE AND HEROISM IN NAZI OCCUPIED HOLLAND

David Groen

authorHOUSE®

AuthorHouse™
1663 Liberty Drive
Bloomington, IN 47403
www.authorhouse.com
Phone: 1-800-839-8640

Published by AuthorHouse 4/4/2012

ISBN: 978-1-4685-7390-9 (sc)
ISBN: 978-1-4685-7389-3 (e)
ISBN: 978-1-4685-7746-4 (hc)

Library of Congress Control Number: 2012905479

FOREWORD

by Rabbi Nardus Groen, of blessed memory

The life that was not lived:

This is the story of two people whose experiences cannot be seen as separated from one another. At the same time, it includes a multitude of people whose story will never be told. We therefore consider it a privilege as well as a duty to share with you some of the 4,380 days of our being on this earth.

Existence is more or less a state of exposure. Life, on the other hand, is a matter of faith. If there was such a thing, my choice would be for something in between. Some attributes may be applied to it, and others may not fit the shoe.

We may in the course of it meet people who, for whatever it's worth, may be portrayed as heroes, while others are cowards, pacifists, or activists. They are all the products of mankind. For them, there will always be a place under the sun (with the exception of the traitor). But being as we are a homogenous society, no one can ever be left out. And as it is by the very inclination of the human race, the dark shadow of the wicked will play an overpowering role in leaving behind the marks in the way of scars brought upon them by society.

If the worst could ever be turned into good, the only lesson to be learned of that is, never ever forget. For in the past lay the present, and in the present the future. Without that, we will be repeating our mistakes and shortcomings, and as a result the world will not be the place it was created to be.

In order to live, you still have to be able to somehow believe in the goodness of mankind. In that light, we will start with our first words to describe that which has been and never should have been.

INTRODUCTION

The story you are about to read is the true account of the lives of Nardus and Sipora Groen. As it would be in any recounting of people's lives, remembering all the details with exact precision is impossible. However, there is not one story, not one act of heroism, and no documentation of someone's direct involvement in historical events that does not have its origin in complete truth.

When the Nazi occupiers marched into Amsterdam in May of 1940, one tenth of the city's population was Jewish. The perception, one based on a strong reality, was that a typical Dutchman during that time had fair hair and a light complexion, while the typical Jew had darker hair and a darker complexion. Those dark features gave Jews in Holland what was to be known as a "*Joden kop.*" The literal translation is "Jewish head," but in essence what this meant was that when you saw this darker skinned person, they had the face of a Jew. Thus, the title of this book, *Jew Face*.

Although most of this story is an account of extraordinary heroism and strength, much of what happened in the lives of both Nardus and Sipora Groen was affected by their respective physical appearances.

What you are about to read, as remarkable as it will seem, truly happened. And now, without further ado, I begin what has been my life's greatest honor: the telling of my parents' story.

PROLOGUE

The date was Friday, August 13, 1943, and it felt like the worst moment of Sipora's young life. She knew that the Germans were in the building and getting closer to finding her. She had already been through so much and she knew that the situation was going to get a lot worse before it got better. Her will to live was being taken over by despair. She was not the type of woman who would ever do anything to speed up her own death, but she also did not feel like running or fighting. So she decided that she would just wait on the third floor and when the Nazi soldiers located her, she would willingly leave with the rest of the patients and hospital staff. At least then she felt as though she could do some good by making the sick and elderly patients a little more comfortable.

Nardus, however, had no intention of allowing this to happen. As had been the case since the beginning of the Nazi invasion of Amsterdam, he instinctively knew that whatever Jews were not murdered instantly would instead suffer greatly through torture, experimentation, rape, or brutal slave labor. Since he found Sipora before the soldiers did, he knew he had to get her out. And to a man like Nardus, it did not matter what Sipora thought of this idea. It was going to happen his way. And that was that.

When Sipora saw Nardus, she had already sunk so deep into hopelessness she wasn't even able to feel any sense of relief. And she was determined to let him know.

"I am just going to wait here and let them take me too," she told

Nardus. "They will need a nurse for the trip. If nothing else, I can make them feel more comfortable."

Some moments define an individual, and other moments can define a relationship between two individuals. In many ways, what was about to take place would define much of Nardus and Sipora's relationship. True to his nature, Nardus was not suggesting or asking what would happen next. What he was doing was telling Sipora what would happen next.

"I'll tell you what," he said in his straight-to-the-point manner, "since you are going to your death anyway, and that is your plan, I will throw you out the window right now myself. At least then you will die quickly. Either way you will die."

Sipora was crying now. "What's the point?" she said. "There's no hope. My family is gone; your family is gone. They're even taking sick and old patients from here and transporting them out of the city."

Knowing that he needed to remain calm and in control, Nardus made it very clear to Sipora what was to happen next.

"Get up and let's get out of here. We will find a way to survive this. All you have to do is trust me and listen to what I tell you to do."

Although what she was experiencing felt like hell, Sipora was at least able to move now. What made the difference was that someone else, someone she was growing to trust more and more by the day, was taking control and leading her in what at least felt like a better direction.

Neither Nardus nor Sipora had any idea what was to come next, but it did not matter. The only thing that mattered now was that Nardus would never allow either one of them to just sit and wait to be killed.

At this moment, which signified all the drama, horror, and significance of the times they were living through, these two people were thrust together in a way that set the tone for all that was yet to come.

ORIGINS

To really grasp the meaning and significance of this story, you first need to accept two important truths about human beings. The first is that they are capable of the most unspeakable and horrific actions—actions that can only be described as evil. The second is that they can be capable of such decency, heroism, and love that much of the time, good triumphs over evil. In order to truly appreciate what you are about to read, you must start by accepting these truths. Truths they are, because what you are going to read here truly happened.

Even today, with all its history, Holland is a nation of relative obscurity to many throughout the world. They know of windmills and wooden shoes, and others may know of its herring and cheeses, but ask many where the nation of Holland is, and they will say somewhere near Denmark (actually it is between Germany and Belgium). Many of those who know that Amsterdam is in Holland might know about the richness in culture represented by numerous museums and historical landmarks. Others just know of its liberal views toward prostitution and drug use. Then there are those who will ask that all-telling question: Is it the same as the Netherlands? Technically, Holland is part of the Netherlands, which encompasses the larger area of land and government.

Holland is a country of Germanic origin. And in 1933, when Nazi Germany rose to power, it was clearly the rise of a large threat to the small nation off the coast of the English Channel. Amsterdam was then, as it is today, a thriving town. However, the difference was that in 1933, approximately 10 percent of Amsterdam's almost 800,000 inhabitants were Jewish. And with the rise of Nazi Germany, that statistic put Holland at even greater risk than it already was. Most of the Jewish population in Amsterdam and throughout the rest of Holland, even if they were aware of what Nazi Germany stood for, were prepared to turn a blind eye and believe that if anything was going to happen, it was going to happen somewhere else.

Nardus Groen was a different type of man, however. Whether it was his position in the family or the tough economic times or just the character traits he was born with, Nardus was in many ways a cold, hard, pragmatic realist. He was also an Orthodox Jew, one with exceptional knowledge of Jewish practices and rituals.

Nardus was born on December 18, 1919, in the port city of Rotterdam. His father, Leendert Groen, stood by his principals and feared nothing when it came to doing what he knew to be right. Nardus was one of five children. He had two older brothers, one older sister, and one younger sister. His parents moved to Rotterdam after they were married but before they had any of their children.

Once they got there, his father opened a paper business. Since they were strict in their practice of Judaism, their store was not open on Saturday, Shabbat, the Jewish Sabbath. When things began to become difficult for everyone owning a business, and the worldwide economy began to falter, it became apparent that keeping the shop closed much of Friday afternoon and on Saturday led to the business failing. This essentially forced the family to pick up and move.

Leendert really did not have much of a decision to make, because under no circumstances was he going to work on Shabbat. So he had no choice but to give up the business, and as an Orthodox Jew with no business left in Rotterdam, the logical next move was to relocate his family to Amsterdam. There at least he knew his children would be exposed to a life with Jewish values on a daily basis.

Maryan Groen was eight years older than her husband. Leendert, who grew up in an orphanage, was an easygoing, hard-working, and intelligent man. In the Groen household, the true rock was the more stoic Maryan. As is true in every family, the dynamic of the parents formed the character and behavior of the children. Suffice it to say that Nardus Groen grew up to be a man of strength, character, and somewhat radical perspectives when it came to how he reacted to the behavior of others. It did not take very long for Nardus to understand the difference between right and wrong.

It was close to a two-and-a-half-hour ride on the train from Rotterdam to Amsterdam. Leendert and Maryan were by this time beyond exhausted. They were traveling with five children, significant luggage, and the burdens of uncertainty following them everywhere. Maryan loved and respected her husband very much. She knew that he had literally done everything in his power to make the business succeed. She also knew that she was with a man who shared her values, one who knew that he needed to not only support his family, but educate and guide them as well.

The Jewish way of life was one of integrity and decency, moral excellence and discipline. Money was always going to be important no matter where they lived, but ultimately, as long as they had a roof over their head and enough food to sustain themselves, they would be fine. This was a general belief they both shared. So Leendert's decision not to compromise his Jewish way of life by opening his shop on Saturday, the Jewish Shabbat, was met with agreement and support by Maryan.

Maryan saw no distress in Leendert's face, yet as they sat in the uncomfortable car of the train moving them all to their new lives, she knew that this was the time to say something to boost his spirits.

"I am so looking forward to arriving in Amsterdam," she said to the husband she admired so much. "The community there is like none other in Holland. It will be so good for the children, and you will be able to make so many friends who think the way that you do."

"I agree with you," he replied. "But it will not be easy. Our lifestyle will change significantly. We will need to be careful with money in a way like never before. I hear that all over Europe and in America, people are struggling just to put food on the table."

"We will be fine, Leendert," Maryan replied reassuringly. "God will provide us with all that we need."

"You know, my wife, that those are words I will never dispute," replied Leendert. "But we are taught that although we need to have faith in God, we are not to rely on miracles. So we need to be careful, and we need to start immediately."

Maryan knew that words like these from an optimistic man of strength and faith were the closest he would come to panic. She knew that Leendert would stay calm, be strong, and provide the family with what was needed. Yet she also knew he was somewhat concerned and that her words had done nothing to alleviate the concerns, because on this generally friendly joyful face was a cold, stoic look, one that gave Maryan confidence, but also one that made her somewhat sad. She wanted her husband to be happy. With all that he gave all of them, he deserved that. And there was really nothing she could do. Because what gave him joy was to give meaning and joy to his wife and to see his children develop into well-adjusted, decent individuals.

The train was about ten minutes outside of Rotterdam.

"Tickets please!" shouted the conductor. "For those buying tickets on the train, please have your cash ready. Thank you very much."

He arrived in front of Leendert, Maryan, and the children, and after determining that they had not yet purchased their tickets, he looked around and made his calculations.

"Okay, I see we have five full-price tickets, and two young ones under six years old at half price."

Young Nardus, who had been quiet the whole trip till now, stood up straight in front of the conductor, and with a smile on his face spoke almost as loud as the conductor had, saying, "I beg your pardon sir, I am six and a half years old."

The conductor was quiet. He seemed uncertain what to do until Leendert helped him out.

"The boy speaks the truth," he said. "I will be paying you six full prices and one half."

The conductor nodded gratefully, completed the transaction, and walked away.

Maryan looked at Nardus and then at Leendert. As she saw her husband looking with pride at his youngest son, she finally glimpsed what she was hoping to see all day. A smile.

As Leendert Groen looked out the window, he realized that with all the difficulties they would face, this was the right move. This was what he wanted for his children. Financial comfort and abundance was nice, but he wanted his children to grow up with values. He had asked God to give him a sign that he was doing the right thing. What his son Nardus had just done was all the proof he needed that to be in an environment filled with piety and knowledge was far more important than material comfort. He was very proud of his young boy and looked out the window with a smile on his face.

They were ready to start their new life.

If you wanted to know what made the Jewish community of prewar Amsterdam special, you really needed to look in two places. The *"Esnoga"* as it was called, was the main Spanish-Portuguese synagogue; it was so rich in stature and elegance that it was as much a Dutch monument as much as it was a Jewish one. It was (and still is) a structure filled with beauty, elegance, sophistication, but most of all history. When the Jewish community was expelled from Spain in 1492, many went to Portugal, but they did not stay long. After a relatively short stay in Portugal, many continued to the north and found a home in Holland, where they were not only able to live freely, they were able to develop and cultivate the Spanish element in their Jewish background, otherwise known as Sephardic Judaism.

The majority of Jews worldwide belong to one of two groups: Sephardic and Ashkenazic. Literally translated, *"Ashkenazi"* means German and *"Sephardi"* means Spanish. Most of the Jews who were dispersed from Germany centuries earlier would end up in countries such as Russia, Poland, and Hungary. The Spanish Jews dispersed not only to Portugal and subsequently Holland, but to North Africa as well. Many great Jewish scholars emerged in these countries, which led to the development of strong Jewish communities in lands such as Morocco, Tunisia, Libya, and Egypt, to name a few.

By far, the most significant Sephardic community after the expulsions from Spain and Portugal formed in Holland, mainly Amsterdam. Combining a rich tradition that consisted of serious ritualism and pomp and circumstance, the Sephardic Jews of Amsterdam developed a sophistication that was to distinguish them from the remainder of the Jewish population.

Services in the Esnoga occasionally drew Jews from all over Amsterdam. Although most congregants were Sephardic Jews, it was not uncommon for Jews from other neighborhoods to participate in the services. After all, the difference between the two elements is based on specific customs as opposed to a difference of legality. So for a practicing Ashkenazi Jew to partake in a Sephardic ritual was not considered a violation of any sort. If anything, it indicated a broader view toward the faith and, in some circles, was considered a positive character trait, one that Nardus and his closest friends possessed.

The other neighborhood that made the Jewish community of Holland special was the Jewish ghetto. In many ways, this was more the heart and soul of Amsterdam Jewry than the Sephardi community. This neighborhood was filled with scholars, synagogues, and the leaders of the Dutch Jewish community. Synagogues were in abundance in this neighborhood, and most of them were filled to capacity on any given Saturday morning in celebration of the Shabbat.

The Jewish community of Amsterdam primarily revolved around the ghetto. It was not an official ghetto, but inasmuch as it was almost entirely Jewish and Orthodox, it might as well have been. This ghetto was located in the heart of the town, not far from some of the city's most important and historical institutions. Growing up in Amsterdam was somewhat of a treat for an Orthodox Jew. There were isolated incidents of anti-Semitism, but for the most part it was a life rich with activity, education, and community experiences. Leendert and Maryan's family fit well in the community, and their five children, Meyer, David, Sofia, Nardus, and Elizabeth, were accepted quickly and with an ease that has always been standard in Orthodox Jewish communities, especially in ghettos.

When Leendert arrived in Amsterdam, he had a reputation of being a devoted, pious man. This was a man who had lost his business in Rotterdam because he refused to be open on the Sabbath. In the days of very Jewish Amsterdam, this was something that elevated you in status, it did not diminish you.

Nardus considered himself fortunate in his education. Because his mother was an educated woman and highly devoted to her family and Judaism, and because his father was a learned and respected man in the community, he would always be learning not only about the laws of the religion, but of the history as well. The education he would receive would benefit him in understanding when something was not right.

Leendert took a job in Amsterdam as a *mashgiach*, someone who supervises the slaughtering and preparation of meat according to the ritual requirements of Judaism. He also has the responsibility of supervising any location that prepares kosher food. Although their lifestyle was significantly diminished from the one they had in Rotterdam, Leendert's job was an important one in this particular community. It allowed him to provide his family with the necessities of life. In those days in Holland, a *mashgiach* was a highly respected and comparatively well-paid profession that allowed the family to reestablish roots with a degree of security and stability.

Nardus had a strong love and respect for his parents, which he maintained his entire life. His father once sat with him and gave him a piece of advice that was indicative of the calm, thoughtful demeanor he always displayed.

The streets where Nardus lived were not closed off to the rest of the world. Most of the people he walked past on a daily basis were Jews, but plenty of non-Jewish people came into the neighborhood on a regular basis.

Anti-Semitism was not a problem in Holland, per se, but that didn't mean it did not exist at all. There were still plenty of people in Holland who saw the Jews as Christ killers or looked at Jews as strange and different. There was no evidence of a rising tide against them, and the average Jew usually did not experience any acts of violence, but there still was the occasional act of anti-Semitism.

When the Nazis occupied the country, it was believed that there were 30,000 fascist sympathizers to their cause. Most of these belonged to the Dutch Nazi party, known as the *Nationaal-Socialistche Beweging* (National Socialist Movement), or NSB. Many of these NSBers, as they were known, were willing collaborators to atrocities that were to later befall the Jewish community.

Nardus's walk from school was forty-five minutes each way, and there was plenty of exposure on a daily basis to people from all different neighborhoods. One day, he was on his way back home when he heard a boy across the street shout, "Oh look, it's the dirty Jew again."

Nardus did not know what to do. He was not scared, but he also did not want to make worse trouble. The boy kept shouting and would not stop. He began running after Nardus. Nardus, who instinctively was not afraid of people, did not run. He stopped, turned around, and said to the boy, "What is it you want from me?"

"You're a dirty Jew," the boy said. "What could I possibly want from you?"

Nardus felt tremendous anger. He was not frightened at all and was very comfortable with the thought of giving this boy a beating. He just might have done so if it hadn't been for the words of his father that were resonating through him at this time.

He walked up to the boy, stood straight and confident in front of him, smiled, and said, "Thank you."

He then turned and walked away from the stunned, motionless boy he had just confronted in a very unconventional manner.

As he continued home, he remembered what his father had taught him.

These were Leendert Groen's words to his son just ten days earlier:

"When a child comes to you and calls you a dirty Jew, you say thank you, and walk away. Don't get mad. It's not his fault. It's what he was taught at home."

These words, words of wisdom, had proceeded to keep Nardus from getting in an unnecessary fight, but what they also did was give him the opportunity to do so without backing down. You see, even at this young age, Nardus was a fighter. And although he had allowed the words of reason to rule this particular situation, backing down from an attack was something Nardus was not prepared to do. Not now, not ever.

Nardus's upbringing was a simple yet meaningful one. His home life was filled with the most devout practices of the Jewish faith; his family did not put any type of significance on wealth or social status. In Jewish ghettos in old Europe, everyone lived as a traditional Jew, and the only way to achieve higher status was to excel in Jewish studies or ritual practices.

Every morning at the crack of dawn, Leendert would take his boys to the synagogue to pray with him. Although he was an easygoing man, when it came to the structure of Jewish life, Leendert Groen believed in strict discipline. To his way of thinking, if you were Jewish, you lived like a Jew. And to him, that meant living according to the laws laid out thousands of years earlier. Dietary laws had no room for compromise. Prayer was to be done three times every day of the week, and his children were to be educated as Jews, particularly the boys. None of the boys were to get greater advantage from this than Nardus.

None of the children were against the Jewish lifestyle mandated by their parents, but Nardus more than the others was particularly fond of it. Intellectually, he found the Jewish lifestyle to be fascinating. He wanted to know as much as he could, and if he were to have his way, he would study it until it became his expertise. Nardus's natural learning abilities only served to help him more with this process.

Nardus went to his classes with an exuberance not common in most children and young adults. The life in the ghetto required him to walk forty-five minutes each direction to his school. Obviously the students who lived distances from the school such as Nardus were not able to walk home for lunch, and subsequently they would bring their lunch with them. Leendert had chosen a Yeshiva with the same strict approach toward the religion as he had, so there was no compromise when it came to any major laws, particularly Kashrut, the Jewish dietary laws. So when Nardus brought his lunch, even though he brought it from his strict Orthodox home, the school policy was to inspect it. Once it was approved by a staff member, Nardus would be able to eat his lunch. And even then, under one condition: No meat was allowed on the premises, only dairy.

Rapenburg Street was the central street of the ghetto; Nardus would walk through it almost every day. It was the street that defined Amsterdam's Jewish ghetto. It was highly populated, filled with synagogues large and small, and abundant with houses of learning, be it for the very young or adults who chose to never stop leaning.

It was also a street with an invisible border that separated the poorer residents of the ghetto from those who lived a slightly more modest lifestyle. The separation was known as the *Waii Gatt*. The southern portion of Rapenburg Street was where the "*Beit Midrash Hagadol*," or "Great Synagogue," was located. This was where Nardus regularly prayed; being someone not only highly committed to Judaism but with a photographic memory, Nardus was to become a very active and important figure, even in his young age, in the Great Synagogue.

Nardus and his siblings were all enrolled in the Jewish schools of the area. Nardus was enrolled in the Yeshiva. Many would use this education as a guide for how to continue their lives and to sustain the Jewish life in the ghetto. For some, however, this would be a springboard for continuing Jewish education that would lead to some form of leadership in the community, be it as an educator or religious leader. To the most exceptional, it was the first step to becoming a rabbi.

Nardus gave every indication at an early age of being one of those select few.

The Dutch hierarchy of the Rabbinate, however, was anything but simple. It was set up in such a way that first you became a teacher, then a judge, then a rabbi.

This is how it went for most. You would start in the Yeshiva as a child. Then you would move to a Yeshiva high school, where you would continue your education.

Once you exhibited significant progress at this level, the powers that be would appoint you to the position of *Darshan*. The literal translation of "*Darshan*" is an explainer. In more realistic terms, it meant that you had reached a status allowing you to teach. Not on the highest level by any means, but certainly on a level significantly higher than the average student.

Once you exhibited consistent competence as a *Darshan* and continued expanding your knowledge base, you would inevitably be promoted to the status and position of "*Dayan*," or "Judge." Once one reached this level, one had earned a degree of actual authority to declare law and custom in the community.

After a certain amount of time, the clergy in training would be anointed with the title of "*Moreh*." "*Moreh*" is the Hebrew word for "teacher," but in this particular instance, it basically meant that you had reached the level of rabbi. But the way things were set up in Holland, an individual needed to exhibit the ability to function as a rabbi in theory before being given the title in actuality.

Once a committee determined that all the criteria in place were satisfied that the apprenticeship was successful, the individual would be declared and appointed as a rabbi.

Being blessed with a photographic memory and exceptional intelligence, Nardus was able to learn at a young age what many people in his community were not able to learn in a lifetime.

By the time he was thirteen, he had memorized the Jewish prayer book, and by the age of eighteen, he had done the same with the first five books of the Bible, otherwise known as the Five Books of Moses. Both were written and studied in ancient Hebrew.

Nardus would frequent the library, not only out of necessity but out of joy. The study of all that was Jewish gave him great pleasure. And the library he would frequent was in the Great Synagogue in Rapenburg Street.

The library was beautiful, organized, clean, and filled with Jewish literature. Being that it was part of the Great Synagogue, it had a special aura for Nardus.

The library was actually on the second floor. The synagogue itself was on the first floor, the main floor of the building. As a twelve-year-old boy, Nardus enjoyed visiting the library very much. Besides the opportunity to read as much as time allowed, he also would have a good time with the caretakers of the facility, Meyer and Becca Roos.

"Good morning, my young friend," was the greeting from Mr. Roos. "How are you feeling today? Looks to me like you might be feeling like a piece of buttercake and a glass of milk."

Nardus smiled from ear to ear. Yes, he had that intellectual way about him, but he was also a twelve-year-old boy coming into what was probably his favorite environment and getting special treatment, which included pastries, from two very special people.

He also had his own little joke going on with them.

"I'll be right over there in the corner," Mrs. Roos would say. "I have my eye on you, Nardus. So don't think you're going to be sneaking any of these books out of here and making your own little library at home."

Nardus knew that she was kidding with him. She would say this, smile, walk over with more buttercake, and say, "Here. This should keep you from going anywhere for the time being."

Nardus loved these people. These were the types of people that made one's childhood special, and later on in life, he would look back at sadness at the fact that with all he was able to do for some, he was not able to do anything for Meyer and Becca Roos. There was nothing in his power that would make it possible to save these people from their death at Auschwitz. All Nardus would have is the memory of two ordinary people who were kind, were generous, and had a great impact on his early years.

Between his exceptional intellectual skills, his strong religious upbringing, and his pleasure in participating in Jewish practices, it was clear that Nardus would continue his education and preparation toward becoming a rabbi. When he was nineteen, the cantor at the largest synagogue in his neighborhood suddenly passed away; there was no one in line to take over his responsibilities. The chief rabbi of Amsterdam, knowing of Nardus's talents and enthusiasm, not only gave the honor to Nardus, he also set up an instructor to make sure he knew all that was part of the services. Nardus spent three months studying intensely to learn everything he needed to know to lead the largest and most knowledgeable community in the country on the holiest days of the year.

These were fun and rewarding times for Nardus. He was able to lead a service for those people who mattered most to him, in a setting and environment that had given his life meaning, education, depth, and fun. There was never much money in their lives, but with all the other benefits he had in his world, money was, for the most part, never missed.

In the late 1930s, the Jewish families of the wealthier communities in Amsterdam often employed women to help in cleaning or taking care of the children. However, as much as these families may have been in better financial shape than others in the city, their ability to be able to afford this was a mystery to many.

It was not till later that it was revealed that these German women were part of what was to be known as the fifth column, German citizens who were sent to infiltrate what was later to be prime real estate in Nazi expansion. Even as events had only begun to develop and unfold, Nardus was already able to identify that something about this was not right. This was just another alarm Nardus had noticed from as early as 1935.

Nardus was, by nature, a man who looked at things differently than the average young man in the Jewish ghetto. Yes, he had this love for Jewish practices, laws, and customs, and yes, he had a thirst for knowledge that was never to be quenched. However, he saw things that many of his peers did not see. And this is what motivated him in 1938 to join the National Guard. Joining the guard was unheard of for a young Orthodox man in Amsterdam. However, he did not do this out of rebellion, but out of a desire to be stronger in lieu of the impending storm he instinctually felt coming from the east. Joining the National Guard was a way for him to feel prepared for whatever may come down the line.

In 1938, when the Nazis started their aggressions against the rest of Europe, Nardus felt, as he once stated, "This was the end of us."

The preparation he received by joining the National Guard at least made him feel like he had somewhat of a fighting chance. It was this instinct that separated him in so many ways from others like him in his community. In many ways, it is the reason he was to not only survive the years ahead, but help others as well.

He knew that he wanted to learn how to use weapons. He felt it was important that he learn how to fight in order to battle the enemy forces he knew would soon be approaching. From 1938 to 1940, the National Guard was a full-time job for Nardus, turning this one-time budding Rabbinical prodigy into a military minded man, one who knew that it would take more than scholarly achievements and intellectual pursuits to survive in the times ahead. He found time between 1938 and 1940 to continue his studies, but the environment he was primarily in was a military environment, not a religious one. The progressive nature of his parents would play a great role in helping Nardus to mix these two elements together in his life.

Although they did not live far from each other, Nardus Groen and Sipora Catharina Rodrigues-Lopes were born into two very different worlds. Sipora (Sippy) was born into the lifestyle and culture of the Dutch secular world.

Sipora was born on January 1, 1922 into what once was considered the Dutch Jewish elite, those descending from the Spanish and Portuguese communities that arrived in Holland over four hundred years earlier. Sipora's life growing up was not primarily a Jewish one. Her father, Marcel, and her mother, Deborah, were certainly proud of their Jewish roots, but they attempted to fill the lives of their two children, Sipora and her younger brother, Abraham, with activities and events that were multicultural. There was greater exposure to music, art, secular literature, and certainly more daily exposure to non-Jewish environments.

The main difference was that while Judaism was part of Sipora's life, for Nardus it was his entire way of life. The likelihood of two people from such different environments ending up together was very small, especially in an era where TV and computers had not yet shrunk the world, as they have today. In some ways, people who lived in different worlds never really had any significant exposure to one another.

Sipora's parents were both very musical. Her mother was a soft, sweet woman who was from an educated, sophisticated background. However, Sipora was not to have the good fortune of having many years with her mother, who died when Sipora was thirteen.

Besides the grief of losing her mother, Sipora also took on much of the chores of the household. She had a greater responsibility for the well-being and development of her brother Abraham, or Bram as he was called. This did not cause even the slightest bit of resentment between the two of them; instead it caused them to become even closer than they already were. Bram had what Sipora always described as a soft character. By no means was this a demeaning description of this gentle young man. Instead, it was a way of describing someone without a bad bone in his body. He was kind, loving, gentle, talented, and intelligent. In many ways, the death of Deborah caused such a change in Marcel that Sipora and Bram needed to stay closer than ever; Sipora developed a closeness with her brother that would stay in her heart forever. Marcel would remain a provider and loving father, yet he would also grieve in ways that would take away from the attention they needed. This caused Sipora in many ways to have to strengthen up emotionally in ways that most children her age did not have to do.

Her father spent less time with the children; he found a housekeeper named Emmy to look after their house on Boiler Street while he was away. Emmy would have a great deal of control as the adult in the household, which she ran while Marcel was away.

When Sipora reached young adulthood, a beautiful young woman with dark complexion, she became engaged to be married. Her fiancé, Hans de Jong, was from a very similar background, Jewish but more secular and from the middle class of Amsterdam society. Sipora very much looked forward to marrying Hans. He was a fine young man, intelligent and charming, and he and Sipora enjoyed each other's company very much. An accountant for the Dutch railroad, Hans would travel daily to the city of Utrecht, about twenty miles from Amsterdam. On his days off, Sipora and Hans would spend time with friends or family, including Hans's sister Hetty, who was a friend of Sipora's; they ice skated in the cold winter months or took bicycle trips outside of Amsterdam. They had very little idea of what was in store for them in the not-so-distant future, and even if they had gotten wind of it, through reports from Germany or German refugees arriving in Amsterdam, the life they lived felt protected and safe to them. In some ways, many Dutch Jews felt the way Sipora and Hans felt: untouchable. Prewar Holland was, for many, a place of innocence, and in Sipora's world, a world not stricken by the poverty present in many other neighborhoods, her relationship with Hans was a relatively uncomplicated and purely romantic one. She seemed destined to go through a smooth courtship, marry, and hopefully build a nice family. All these hopes and dreams would take place, of course, in a perfect world, which was the furthest thing from what was to come.

THE RISE OF EVIL

For most people in this community, the world was a small, enclosed space that was filled with all they would ever need, and the thought that anything would disrupt this was inconceivable. However, because of his astuteness and his natural inclination toward a harsh and even unpleasant realism, Nardus knew that their lives had the potential to change very quickly in horrifying and profound ways.

With the rise of the openly anti-Semitic Nazi Party in Germany, many German Jews found a way to get out, and with the Netherlands immediately to their west, this was the most logical place to go. The Jewish communities of Amsterdam helped develop a small area of land in the northern part of Holland so that those who needed to had an adequate place to live. This refugee camp was known as Westerbork. The Jewish families that had come in from Germany mentioned what was going on there, but being that they had left prior to the worst events taking place, even they could not give an account of what was to come. What they did do, however, was to strengthen the preparation of those individuals such as Nardus, who were willing to face the realities, no matter how harsh.

Nardus never considered himself a pessimist. It was more so that he saw things that people were not willing to see. He remembered Neville Chamberlain's glorious statement of "Peace in our time." Nardus knew this was not real. He knew the type of people they were dealing with, and he knew of the hatred that the Jewish people were exposed to.

It was clear to him that the world was turning a blind eye to what was really going on in Nazi Germany. The failed policy of appeasement was allowing German leadership time and space to build the gas chambers that would later be used to exterminate millions, including six million Jews.

The actual number of Dutch Jews murdered in the time of Nazi rule was considerably smaller than in many other countries in Europe, but the percentage of Dutch Jews murdered was not. Prior to 1940, it was estimated that Holland had approximately 140,000 Jews, and by the time it was all over, the Jewish community of this small western European nation was left with not much more than 30,000 survivors.

Nardus had heard the stories. He would frequently spend time in the home of his sister, Fie (Sofia), and her husband, Jacques Baruch, a man who was to play a larger role in Nardus's life in days to come. While visiting, Nardus heard stories from the German family staying with the Baruchs after being forced out of their home in Berlin. In his words, "people had eyes but did not see, and they had ears but could not hear." And later on in retrospect, he felt that if the world had been more aware of what was truly going on and had been more willing to open their eyes to the realities and horrors, they could have prevented the murder of countless millions, including the six million Jews murdered by the Nazis.

While many in the community were stuck in a state of denial or paralysis from fear, Nardus felt more of a resolve and understanding. It was not an acceptance. He was in no way going to accept the events that were unfolding; he was prepared to do whatever necessary to help the lives of those around him while doing his best to ensure his own safety. The National Guard had provided him an education in self-defense that included the use and possession of multiple weapons, including a firearm. And if necessary, he would certainly be willing to use whatever means necessary for his and his loved one's protection.

IT'S WAR

Sipora's father, Marcel, was by no means oblivious to what was going on in Europe. So when the German war machine was ready for Holland, he knew what was happening.

It was 4:30 the morning of May 10, 1940, and being that it was springtime, the first signs of daylight had begun. Sipora was suddenly awakened by the sound of airplanes flying overhead. A young woman of only eighteen, she was clueless as to what this really meant, and all she felt was curiosity and confusion.

Like so many Dutchmen who were aware of what was happening in other parts of Europe, Marcel Rodrigues had a good idea of the intentions of the Nazi war machine.

"They want to throw us all in the Zuider Zee (South Sea)," he said, a statement that was not literally accurate, but was sadly prophetic in substance.

So that morning when the planes were flying overhead, on a night when Sipora heard sounds she had never heard before, she asked her father what was going on. He was to answer her in a very distinct, yet uncharacteristically cold way, and very accurately said to his daughter Sipora, "It's war."

It turned out that the German planes were on their way to Rotterdam. The Nazis used the invasion and subsequent bombing of Rotterdam as a weapon to make the Dutch capitulate, warning that if they did not, the city of Amsterdam would be destroyed much as they had destroyed most of the inner city of Rotterdam. Ironically, by the time Rotterdam had been bombed, the Dutch government had already fallen.

Rotterdam had to be entirely rebuilt, effectively making it one of the most modern cities in postwar Holland. Amsterdam, however, was not bombed at all and, to this day, still maintains much of its older architecture.

The Dutch government, although friendly, was powerless against the German war machine. On May 10, 1940, the Nazis invaded Holland. Five days later, the country was entirely under German control.

The Dutch royal family and government ministers escaped into exile in England. The Dutch government, headed by Prime Minister Dirk Jan de Geer, was invited back by the Germans to remain in power under control of the Nazi Party. De Geer wanted to accept the proposal but was overruled and removed by Queen Wilhelmina, who had no intention of cooperating with the invading force. She replaced de Geer with Pieter Gerbrandy, who in turn officially refused the Nazi invitation to return and run the new Nazi government in Holland. With the Dutch government removed and living in exile, a German governor was appointed to supervise policy, and a civil government, led by Arthur Seyss-Inquart, an Austrian, was installed.

In the immediate days following the outbreak of the war in Holland, Sipora's father took all their Jewish books and threw them down a well, in the hope that it would help to save his family. He understood that the Jewish people were in danger, but what he was not able to see was that at this point, the Nazis had already put together such an efficient information and killing machine that hiding the fact that you were Jewish was next to impossible without changing your identity and having a more Dutch appearance than a Jewish one.

Most Sephardic Jews, including Sipora as well as her father and brother, had the dark features that were considered the typical Jewish look. Holland at the time was not a nation of immigrants as it is today, so that the complexion of the skin and color of the hair, primarily in Amsterdam, represented to many the distinction between Jew and non-Jew. To have the dark hair and the browner skin meant that you had the face that could only belong to a Jew, and that meant you were easily identifiable by friend and foe alike.

ASSAULT ON THE COMMUNITY

It wasn't till the first days of February 1941 that significant incidents of persecution against Dutch Jews began to take place. Angered by growing acts of anti-Semitism in their neighborhood, a group of men from the Rapenburg Street area got into many physical altercations with NSBers.

With the world economy in shambles, governments throughout Europe were in flux, with some even in the midst of radical change toward fascism and totalitarian rule. Along with Hitler's Germany came Mussolini's Italy and Franco's Spain. Although there was no deposing of the government or monarchy in Holland, the wave of fascism that hit Europe found some traction in Holland as well. In 1931, led by Anton Mussert, the National Socialist Movement of the Netherlands was founded. When the Nazis occupied Holland in 1940, the NSB would remain the only legal political party in Holland.

For the Jews of Holland, this presented an additional problem to an already troublesome situation. It was clear who the Germans were and that their intentions toward the Jewish population were hostile, but now there was the concern of whether or not the ordinary Dutchman could be trusted. Having Nazi sympathizers to contend with only made it that much more dangerous.

On February 12, 1941, as a response to these altercations, the local Nazi government formed the "*Joodsche Raad*" or "Jewish Council," a committee led by Jews to oversee activities in the Jewish community.

A LOST COUSIN

After her mother died, five years prior to the occupation, Sipora would find solace in whatever support she could from close friends and family. Everyone meant well, and there were people who came by the house often, but between the tough economic times and the fact that people had their own families to attend to, it was difficult for most to come see her, her brother, and her father on any consistent basis.

Sipora was always well mannered and gracious and always showed the appropriate appreciation toward anyone who helped her or her family. Like anyone else, though, Sipora had her favorites. These were the people whose visits brought genuine joy. One such person was her cousin David Van Hasselt.

David wore that special mantle of favorite cousin. He had been a regular visitor in their household for years and had every intention of coming at least as often, if not more, after the untimely passing of Sipora's mother. Sipora loved his visits. He would make her laugh; he would talk with her about music, art, ice skating; and he would even help her with her schoolwork from time to time. Whenever he would visit, it would be the highlight of her day.

After her mother died, Sipora needed anything that made the day a little special. At the young age of thirteen, Sipora had household responsibilities thrust upon her most often given to women at least five years older. Her life at a young age was not easy. Her cousin David was a special friend.

David Van Hasselt was a bright, funny, strong young man, who at the outbreak of war in Europe had made the decision to join the Dutch army. On May 15, five days after the Germans attacked, the war was over in Holland. With the Nazis steamrolling through Holland and Belgium and bearing down on France, the Allies planned a defensive assault on Dunkirk, France. If nothing else, it was an attempt to slow down, if not halt, the German juggernaut. So it was on May 24, 1940, fourteen days after the war had begun and nine days after the war was over in Holland, that David Van Hasselt was amongst the Allied troops confronting the Nazis in what would be a failed attempt at any sort of conquest.

Although the mission at Dunkirk was a failure, a total disaster was averted when Nazi leadership chose to delay any counterattack for three days in an effort to maintain solid control of its forces. This gave most of the Allied forces time to regroup and evacuate to England.

David, however, chose to go back to his hometown of Amsterdam rather than follow the other soldiers to England. Having all his family and friends in Holland, David felt that the only correct choice for him would be to go back home and be with the people he cared about.

Meanwhile, the Nazi occupiers of Holland, who until now had taken no action against the Jewish population, were getting geared up to make their first raid against what they saw as this inferior race. They planned to hit in the heart of the Jewish community of Amsterdam, sending troops to Rapenburg Street in the center of the Jewish ghetto. Their orders were to pick up between 300 and 500 young, healthy Jewish men for deportation. They wanted to create immediate fear and doubt in those who were most able or likely to oppose them in future attacks, while fabricating a claim of an imposing threat.

David was not a resident of the Jewish ghetto, but a number of people that he was close to did indeed live there. One such person was his sweetheart, who he would visit on a regular basis. The past few weeks had been better times for David than any he had seen since before the war. He had enjoyed the time with his parents, caught up with his best friends, and now was on his way to Rapenburg Street to see his girl. They had been discussing their plans for the future, and although things were not looking very good for Europe as a whole, life had to go on, and being with her was the only way David wanted it to be at this time. They had considered going to England together in the assumption that things on the

Continent were going to get worse before they would get better. They had discussed it many times and hoped that if it was necessary, they would be able to leave together.

On February 22, 1941, as David was walking on Rapenburg Street, he heard what sounded like screaming and fighting. When he turned the corner, he saw a mob of what looked like a thousand people; the majority was the Grune Polizei (Green Police). He knew he could do nothing and was considering turning around or hiding. But it was too late. They had already seen him.

Sipora's favorite cousin was one of those taken away to Mauthausen in the raid of February 1941. David did not make it out, and would spend the next 7 months in the concentration camp before a report came back saying that he had died. When Sipora's uncle learned of his son's demise, he knew he needed to let his daughter know about her brother's fate. However, being that his wife was no longer with him, he would have to tell her alone. This was something he could not do. He needed the help of someone close to him, and he needed it to be a woman. So he asked Sipora to help him. Sipora, at the age of nineteen, was already experiencing more death than most people would by that age. The lessons she learned at a young age would help see her through even more difficult times and teach her in many ways how to transfer that strength to the people close to her. However, as the war broke out, the first feeling for her, as it was for so many, was terrifying despair. And to have to break the news of the death of someone she loved so much to another relative she was so close with was in itself a horror she had not yet experienced. Especially considering the circumstances, or at least as much as she knew about the circumstances surrounding his death.

David Van Hasselt: Murdered September 16, 1941, Mauthausen.

The entire chain of events that resulted in the raid and deportation of these Jewish men, including Sipora's cousin David, appeared to be a setup from the start. Soon after the Jewish Council was formed, an NSBer was shot in what was said to be an altercation with some militants fighting back against the Nazi occupation. In retaliation for his murder,

Nazi officials rounded up between 300 and 500 Jewish men and deported them to the concentration camp of Mauthausen. Although the number of people picked up was relatively small, it was essentially the first stage in the systematic destruction of nearly all of Holland's Jewish population.

The outrage of the local Dutch citizenship was severe; a labor strike was organized by local labor union leaders. This resulted in thousands staying away from work and marching in protest against what they considered to be unlawful and unjust treatment of their fellow Dutchmen.

Although the strike would be remembered as courageous and decent, it had no impact on the Nazi occupiers other than to create anger against the elements showing support for the Jews of Amsterdam.

The Nazi response was to execute the organizers of the strike; soon after, they outlawed any other political party other than the NSB.

Although the war broke out in Holland in May of 1940, the onslaught against the Jewish population in Holland was a much slower process. The German strategy in Holland was different from what it was in other nations. They felt that the Dutch were more Aryan than the people in countries such as Poland or Russia, and subsequently they looked to attempt to have the population align with them rather than pummel them into submission. This meant that even the Jewish issue was handled differently. In an attempt to make it appear less brutal to the average Dutchman, the onslaught against the Jewish population was slower and more deliberate.

As the Nazis took more and more control of the streets of Amsterdam, the intimidation of the Jews would increase as well. Later in 1941, after the initial deportation of Dutch Jews and the failed labor strike, a town hall meeting was called by the Jewish Council in the Diamond District in order to hear what was being called "an urgent announcement and stern warning to the local shop owners from the ruling government."

The announcement went something like this:

"You are hereby told, and do not forget, to immediately turn in all your firearms and assault weapons."

Trying to stay abreast of what was taking place, Nardus went to hear the announcement. He knew this was a deceptive and somewhat nonsensical ploy on the part of the Germans. It appeared to be another form of intimidation and a way of justifying the deportation of hundreds of Jewish men weeks earlier. Nardus knew that the Jews of Holland did not own weapons. In fact, having joined the National Guard, he had achieved an almost celebrity status in his community. For a young Jewish man in the Amsterdam of the 1930s to sport a military uniform was something hardly ever seen and made many very proud of him. It was this training, however, that made Nardus even more aware of what the Nazis were doing. This was psychological warfare against the Jews in order to prevent as many as possible from moving in any militant direction. The idea was to create fear of taking action. This mental manipulation was a strategy that, in its success, contributed to the community's devastation.

Nardus knew what was going on. He saw how the Nazis were controlling every aspect of what was taking place in Amsterdam, primarily within the Jewish community. They were setting up courts, tribunals as it were, to deal with what they referred to as troublemakers within the Jewish community. The Jews of the community were made to register, and by June of 1942, every Jew was required by law to wear the infamous yellow star stating that they were Jews.

More and more people from the Jewish community were starting to disappear. Some were taken away openly. At this stage, many were being taken to Mauthausen. Westerbork, the camp that had been set up to help fleeing German Jews, was turned into a full-fledged concentration camp and became an important part of the Nazi plans for Dutch Jewry.

JACQUES

We know that all the tales of war and tragedy throughout history are teeming with villains looking to achieve power or acceptance within the governing body of the aggressor or persecutor. We also know that often, even more than opposing military forces, it is the hero who stands in the way of the evil force achieving the ultimate goal of total destruction or oppression. Some of these heroes throughout time have saved nations and races, while others have saved worlds, one person at a time.

During the Nazi occupation of Europe, the villains and heroes were more pronounced and very easily distinguished. As time goes on, history can turn into fable or legend. The further we get from the time an event took place, the more difficult it becomes to relate to the behaviors of just one heroic individual.

The events that took place in Holland and the rest of Europe during the time of Nazi rule are not merely a story, but an historical account of what really took place. The evil, inhumane behavior of the Nazis is not a fabrication that stems from the mind of the person documenting this; it is an actual account of real events that took place. As hard as it may be to fathom that people can actually behave in this fashion, sadly they did. And the world knows what took place as a result.

However, as hard as it can be to believe that man can be guilty of such evil and cowardice, there also exists that opposing force of bravery and courage that in some ways is just as difficult to comprehend. Decency and kindness are elements of human behavior that exist even in the worst environments. However, when presented with the greatest evils, the most severe consequences, and the most horrifying outcomes, it is that rare individual that rises to the top and exhibits behaviors and actions that often they themselves do not even realize they are capable of performing. In Holland during the years of the Nazi occupation, those individuals who were amongst that special brand of human being would be more apparent and more pronounced. For one reason above all others: They were so desperately needed.

Jacque Baruch was one of the special individuals of this time. Jacque had a close relationship with the Groens; he was considered part of the family from a very young age. As he got older, he fell in love with Sofia, Nardus's older sister, and eventually they married. Jacque's best friend was David Groen, one of Nardus's two older brothers, but in all the years he had known him, Nardus had come to see Jacques as one of his best friends as well. With the close relationship Nardus had with David, his relationship with Jacques would become greater as years went by. And with the warmth and respect Jacques had for the entire family, which very much included Leendert and Marjan, the relationship between Jacques and Nardus would always remain strong. Having lost his father at a young age, Jacques saw Leendert Groen as somewhat of a father figure for him, making his relationship with the entire family even more close and personal.

Jacques became active in the Resistance that had formed in Amsterdam, just as Nardus did. Fighting the Nazis head on would be suicide, but the role they both played was similar during the years of occupation. That role was to save as many people as possible. In one particular situation, one even helped save the other.

Jacques was also one of those people who knew, just as Nardus did, that the events that had unfolded till now were only a preview of what was to come. Things were just beginning to get bad, and they were going to get a lot worse before they got better. Jacques and Sofia had the benefit of insight given to them by the German family they had taken into their home. Having fled Germany a few years earlier, the family told them stories of what was taking place in their former homeland and the brutality that the Nazis displayed on a daily basis. Life for the Jews in Germany had been made unbearable, and it was becoming more and more clear that it was the Nazi plan to dissolve the Jewish community one way or another.

Now that they were in Holland, it was evident that their intentions were to do the same. The process was a bit slower and more deliberate, but the treatment and tactics were almost identical.

The raids were becoming more frequent, with more and more young Jewish men being picked up and transported out of Amsterdam. Many of those that were picked up were not sent directly to Mauthausen, they were sent to the city of Amersfoort, another location for deportation as an internment/transit camp. Word had gotten out that the conditions in Amersfoort were horrific. Once there, many were beaten and tortured, while those not experiencing that initial suffering were starved while waiting final transport to what would be their death in Mauthausen.

In one of the raids in the latter part of 1941, Aaron Mozes, the fiancé of Nardus's younger sister Elizabeth, was picked up and sent to Amersfoort. Both Jacques and Nardus knew that Aaron, already a frail and gentle young man, would not be able to survive there for long.

When anyone was picked up by the Nazis to be taken to another location, such as Amersfoort, it had to be assumed that they were not meant to come back. Jacques was aware of this and would use whatever resources he had at his disposal to get his sister-in-law's fiancé back to Amsterdam. At least then he would have a fighting chance. If not, Jacques was certain that Aaron, if he survived the stay in Amersfoort, would end up dead in Mauthausen.

Somehow, through the use of his growing underground contacts and a superhuman effort, Jacques managed to secure Aaron's release from Amersfoort. It was next to impossible to have anyone return once they had been taken from Amsterdam. Most had already been killed or were to be killed soon after. Yet here were Nardus and Jacques, waiting at Central Station for the train from Amersfoort, on which Aaron was returning from what had not so long ago seemed like a hopeless situation. Aaron Mozes, at this moment at least, seemed to be one of the lucky ones.

The train was emptying out, and Nardus could not seem to locate his future brother-in-law. Jacques grabbed Nardus's arm and said, "Look over there," with a tone of alarming concern. "That man over there, could that be Aaron?"

With all that had already taken place since the occupation began in May of 1940, the first time Nardus was to witness firsthand the horrors awaiting the Jewish people of Amsterdam was right here at Central Station, when he realized that the man Jacques had pointed out to him was indeed Aaron. The young man he was looking at, the man he was almost unable to recognize, looked ragged and destroyed. He was hardly able to walk, his face was gaunt and colorless, and the expression in his eyes was lifeless. The face that till now he knew as that of the man in love with his little sister was now the face of the harsh realities of the new world they would be confronted with on a regular basis.

Nardus and Jacques, standing on each side of him, took an arm and helped Aaron walk out of the station. As they began to walk home, Aaron's lips were quivering. He was trying to speak.

Nardus and Jacques stopped so they could listen to the faint and strained voice of this devastated young man.

"Please," Aaron said with the tone of a sad and hungry beggar. "Please, all I want is a piece of cake."

SAVING NETTIE

As the Germans were to come in on various occasions and raid neighborhoods, the Jewish community in Amsterdam became smaller and more dispersed. Those either not willing to accept the evidence or whose innate courage prevented them from leaving their home would ultimately find themselves shipped off to what we now know would ultimately be their cruel treatment in concentration camps, and in most cases, death.

Throughout 1941, Seys-Innquart, Aus der Funten, and his other henchmen were in the process of determining a location to use as a deportation center for the Jews of Holland. The two most logical places were the *Esnoga*, the Great Spanish-Portuguese Synagogue, and the Hollandse Schouwburg, the great concert hall of Amsterdam. After reviewing it carefully, the Nazis felt that the Schouwburg was the more logical choice. Because of the large amount of Jewish patronage over the years, the proximity to the Jewish ghetto, and the purpose in which it was now going to be used, the Nazis changed its name to the *Joodse* Schouwburg and prepared it for use as a deportation center.

The plan had in many ways already been put into action. The concentration camps of Westerbork and Vugt were set up in the north and south, respectively, and beginning in January of 1942, after mass roundups, Jews were no longer allowed to live anywhere in the Netherlands but Amsterdam or the two camps. When arriving in Amsterdam, these people would either live in the homes of others or would reside in public institutions such as schools or hospitals.

The Schouwburg had been set up and was used for *Straf Gevaals* ("S Cases") and for whatever group of random Jews the Nazis chose to keep there until deportation.

Meanwhile, the death camps of Auschwitz and Sobibor were close to operating at full capacity. The Germans were taking the process of eliminating the Jewish population of Europe to a new level. Once they reached that stage, in July of 1942, the system in which they handled the Jews of Holland was cut and dry. Homes and institutions were raided, and if not emptied out in full, they were left devastated and in shambles. Most of the people picked up in these raids were brought to Westerbork, where they would stay for a short while, days at most, before being transported to the death camps. Those not sent to Westerbork went through Vugt. The majority of the remaining was first processed in the Schouwburg and then went through the same pattern of Auschwitz or Sobibor via Westerbork.

Even before the mass deportations of July of 1942, the *Grune Polizei* ("Green Police"), the Nazi police force patrolling Amsterdam, would make regular raids and roundups in Jewish neighborhoods. Many of the Jews who had an understanding of what was taking place went into hiding before they were forced to leave their homes. For many, this was the reason they survived, although, as was the case with everyone who hid, some were more fortunate than others.

The situation in Amsterdam was worsening from week to week. Thousands of people had already been taken from their homes, and it was becoming more and more clear that this was going to get a lot worse before it got better.

Most of the people being seized from their homes at this point were individuals. Families and couples appeared to be spared for a large part, but it was a tenuous situation at best, and the future had a very ominous feel to it.

One day early in 1942, Nardus was approached by one of his good friends, Sam Abram. Sam lived close to Nardus, and they had attended Yeshiva together, frequented the same gatherings, and knew and liked each other very much. Sam had a younger sister, Nettie, and he was concerned that this young, attractive, single woman would be in danger of being sent to one of the camps. And his fears were justified. Many of the women in the neighborhood had disappeared, and with the incidents of brutality leaking out, no one wanted to spend too much time imagining what this meant. They just knew that is wasn't good. So Sam asked Nardus if he had a way to help Nettie stay out of the camps and remain in Amsterdam.

There was really only one way Nardus could help her: He had to marry her. In so doing, he would at least be able to delay her capture. So Nardus and Nettie Abram were married in an effort to save her life, and for now it appeared to be working. As a married woman, she was able to remain in Amsterdam long enough to allow her to find a family where she could hide. And once the Nazis started taking everyone away, married or not, Nettie would need that hiding place.

Nardus and Nettie remained married through the entire war. Any resolution to the situation would not be able to take place before the war would end. Nardus knew this but did not care. Marital status meant nothing right now. What mattered was saving as many lives as possible. Right now, he had the chance to save the sister of a good friend, and he would do so. What he did wasn't much, and it gave no assurances for the future, but it gave her a chance. Nettie would be safe, at least for now.

THE SCHOUWBURG

There are moments in everyone's life that define who they are and what makes them great. For some people, the ones who rise above that level of mediocrity, these moments are more frequent and come at different times.

When you examine these moments, you will often see that whether it is integrity, intellectual accomplishment, or (as in the story you are about to read) courage, the moment not only lives on with the person throughout their life, in its very greatness, it immortalizes them.

During the time of the Nazi occupation, practically everyone in Amsterdam who was arrested or rounded up by the Nazis was transferred to the Hollandse Schouwburg, a concert hall.

This venue was Amsterdam's equivalent to New York's Carnegie Hall or London's Royal Albert Hall. It was a grand building that had been filled throughout the years with culture and beauty. In its time, the Hollandse Schouwburg was a wonderful place to spend an evening. It was abundantly rich with the highest quality operas, concerts, and shows, and was *the* place for events in Amsterdam.

Nardus had never been in the Schouwburg because the life he had growing up was more isolated to the Jewish community. Almost by definition, Jewish ghettos were always more limited to events that revolved around Jewish culture. He had, however, seen it many times in passing, since it was located just a very short distance from where he lived. Ironically, the events that were to take place would connect him to the old Hollandse Schouwburg in a way that no one else in history would ever be connected.

Within the Jewish community, it was well known that Nardus was involved in underground activities and was doing whatever he could to obstruct the mission of the German occupiers. Being that he looked more Dutch than Jewish, Nardus was able to walk the streets with more freedom than many others. When someone needed help within the Jewish community, Nardus was often the one to be notified. Between his National Guard background and his relative freedom of movement, Nardus often became the logical choice when someone needed help.

One day in early 1942, Nardus heard that a couple would need his help in finding safe haven. The woman who contacted him was someone he knew well and knew to be trustworthy. What she told Nardus was not an uncommon story. This Jewish couple was on the run, Nazi soldiers were closing in on them, and the people needed to be saved; only Nardus could see them to safety. She gave him an address, said she was handing the couple over to him, and told him to hold them overnight until a representative of the underground came to pick them up early the next morning.

However, something went terribly wrong. The woman who called him had either been fed incorrect information or had shared this secret with the wrong person; neither Nardus nor the unfortunate couple were to make it to morning in the house.

Around eight o'clock that night, the house was surrounded by SS soldiers. Somehow they knew about the couple and were ready to take them away, as they had previously done with so many of Amsterdam's Jewish community; they also knew about Nardus as well and immediately placed him under arrest for providing aid to fugitives and what they deemed an act of sabotage. Not knowing that he was a Jew, the Nazi soldiers took him into custody and designated him as a "Straf Gevaals" or "Special Case."

A few days later, word got out that the Jewish woman who had notified Nardus was married to a non-Jewish man by the name of Block. It was

Block who had notified the Germans. Little did Nardus know that he and the couple he was escorting were walking into a trap. The couple was taken to a different location, and Nardus was taken directly to the Schouwburg.

The Dutch underground, through information provided by Jacques Baruch, were notified of what had happened and how Nardus had walked into a trap set by Block. It was never spoken of, but three days later, Block was found with a bullet in his head.

When the SS took Nardus to the Schouwburg, he saw it was guarded by soldiers in front while a truckload of people, almost entirely Jews, was being unloaded. Nardus knew some of these Jews, while many others were either from the provinces outside of Amsterdam or Special Cases such as himself. Day and night, there were transports in and out of the Schouwburg. The ones coming in had been taken from their homes forever. The ones leaving were being transported to the death camps, where an estimated104, 000 Dutch Jews would eventually perish.

Partially in order not to be recognized and partially in order not to see an image that would possibly haunt him forever, Nardus kept his head low. As the people were being moved inside, Nardus heard the buzz of people who were already there. But this was not the sound of concertgoers anxiously anticipating a performance of beauty. There were to be no more nights of beauty and culture in this building. The Nazis had transformed what was once a building of culture and elegance into a building of horror and tragedy. They had turned it into a central location for the transportation of people they had picked up for processing before they were to be shipped off to concentration camps. Since the intentions of the Germans were sinister, they had no concern for the conditions of the people waiting for transportation. They did not care whether there was ample facility to sit, sleep, eat, rest, or even be provided the basic dignities of cleanliness.

The majority of the people being held there were Jewish, except for a smaller percentage who were being held there as "Special Cases" (or "S Cases"). These were individuals who were considered unsympathetic or even active against the Nazi regime and occupation. They were, by the German standards of that time, criminals. Nardus was considered by the Nazis to be one of these individuals. One of the major differences between the Jewish prisoners and the Special Cases was that the latter were required to stand trial. The Jews were being held under the pretense of relocation, but the S Cases were there for "crimes" and therefore had to be dealt with judicially.

The school across the street from the Schouwburg was now being used by the Nazis as an impromptu courthouse. Their so-called tribunals were being held there as formalities before they sent someone across the street to wait shipment to a camp. The trials that were held were primarily for the S Cases, and to the Nazis, cause for suspicion was enough reason to find someone guilty. They were not at all concerned with whether or not an innocent man was being sent to die, because they felt any non-German was expendable. Nardus knew this was the case and realized that the less he said the better. He had an image in his head of a group of serious, harsh, stern officials waiting to drop their judicial hammer on anyone that rubbed them the wrong way. So needless to say, Nardus was shocked when he was brought into a room of drunk and disorganized German officers. It had more the appearance of a poker game than a jury. They were laughing, smoking, and drinking, and clearly had been doing so for many hours. There was not a sober one in the entire group. Nardus stood there with a very neutral, unrevealing expression. He certainly had no intention of showing the contempt he felt, but he also knew that talking and laughing with them would be a mistake as well. And since this was something that he never ever had any desire to do with anyone wearing a Nazi uniform anyway, he just stood there with an empty expression. He would choose a firing squad before he would ever pretend to be one of these murderers' friends.

They took his ID card from him, which read "Cornelius Gugjes."

"Hey you! Komme hier," commanded the head of the tribunal. "Why are you here?"

Nardus knew that his answer to this question, especially in the German's current condition, would be critical. He also knew that the one advantage he had over the large number of Nazi officers surrounding him was that his mind was clear and focused.

"I am not really sure," he replied. "I think they have me confused with someone else."

Hollandse Schouwburg

In a drunken slur, the commandant shouted to Nardus, "How do you plead?"

In the most convincing tone he could possibly muster up, Nardus declared with total confidence, "Not guilty."

Between the commanding certainty in Nardus's voice and the alcoholic stupor the German officers found themselves in, something must have worked.

"Give me back his papers!" ordered the commandant. "Not guilty!" he shouted and stamped it on Nardus's papers. "Now be on your way!"

Nardus was more than happy to obey this command and left this room full of men ready to pass out from intoxication.

Nardus knew that he had just dodged a bullet, but he also knew that he was not out of the woods yet. He had a very serious problem. It was now after eleven, the curfew was in effect until six o'clock, and he knew that leaving the building would only lead to him being picked up all over again.

Nardus found a quiet corner and rested in the hope that by the following morning, he would be able to leave undetected and make his way to a safe location.

The problem was that there was no real place to hide in this school now turned courthouse, and the appearance of hiding might only bring unwanted attention, which meant that he was much more out in the open than he would have liked.

Unfortunately, what started as an incredible stroke of good luck turned terribly wrong when, at 4:30 in the morning, Nardus heard the steps of angry soldiers approaching.

They saw him sitting quietly in the corner and shouted, "On your feet, boy! The commandant wants to see you again."

Nardus was marched back into the room where his original "hearing" took place. The atmosphere was different now. For what had started off as a bunch of drunk, half asleep, somewhat happy drunk German soldiers was now a room of wide awake, hung over, angry officers. The alcohol had worn off and the officers, having had enough presence of mind to know that Nardus had been there, called him back, changed their mind, and stamped his papers "Guilty."

Just as he had been found innocent on a whim, the process of finding Nardus guilty was just as swift and illogical.

Logical or not, the end result was the same, and Nardus was sent back across the street to the Schouwburg as a man guilty of crimes against the Third Reich, awaiting deportation to a concentration camp.

The Schouwburg seated approximately 500 people. The Nazis had set it up in such a fashion so that the people awaiting transport were in the main gallery, while the people in the balcony were members of the Jewish Committee, whose function was to help the Germans run the facility. These people were more fools than they were traitors because although they did not take part in atrocities against their fellow Jews, they were under the misguided perception that by helping the Germans administratively, they would be spared the fate of the others.

In the main gallery, there were men and women of all ages, sick people, little children, and babies. Nardus could not tell how many people were actually in the Schouwburg, but he knew that they were being pushed in there without any concern for comfort or health.

The process by which the Nazis conducted the deportation was to call out the names of the people when they were ready to ship them out. At first, many of the Dutch Jews were transported to Westerbork, the concentration camp in Holland. Later, they would be shipped to the Dutch city of Amersfoort, where they also had a midway house set up. Ultimately, they would ship everyone to Sobibor and Auschwitz, where almost all of them were murdered in gas chambers.

Nardus understood very well that the next place he would go was not going to be a good one, and therefore he had no intention of making it easy on the Germans.

When he was in the Schouwburg, Nardus was startled by what he saw and heard. The fear and naiveté of the people led them to actually believe the German phrase, "Ardbeid Makt Frei," translated into English, "Work Makes Freedom." Nardus looked around the Schouwburg. Yes, he saw young, strong people in the room, but he also saw a large number of children, infants, old people, and sick people. He thought to himself, "These people are going to work?" This was not right. He knew the real intentions of the Nazi war machine and had no intention of falling for this tragic ruse.

There really needed to be a new word to describe the deplorable conditions in the Schouwburg. As they were doing all over Europe, the Nazis were treating people, primarily Jews, as subhuman. The Germans had no concern for the health and well-being of the people being held there and certainly were not concerned about the conditions in the room from a hygienic standpoint.

Nardus knew that he had to take care of himself while he was there. He also knew that he was either going to remain there indefinitely, or he was going to get out. After he had been there two weeks, they called his name to be transported out, most likely to Auschwitz. He had no intention of going to the death camp. He managed to get a few slices of bread here and there to stay alive, and in order to not be detected when called, he hid under the mattresses of others waiting transportation. Being walked on and being exposed to unsanitary conditions was still better than being shipped off to a camp.

Since the hall had been overloaded beyond comfortable capacity, Nardus was able to remain undetected for close to seven weeks. However, he knew that he had to get out of there. Staying there much longer was not a viable option, because he knew if he was not found, he would eventually succumb to either hunger or disease. Nardus was not hiding to die slower;

he was hiding in order to keep going. And that was what he had every intention of doing.

Nardus would roam around the hall at times when the transportation activities had slowed down to a quiet pace. German soldiers were either sleeping, drunk, or disinterested, and the only areas that were not free to walk around were near the front or rear doorways.

Nardus was standing in one of the back corners when he heard a hissing sound coming from within earshot and then someone whispered, "Nardus, come here."

He recognized this man as Jan Coopman, a comrade from the National Guard. However, Jan was not a prisoner, he was dressed as some sort of night guard or watchman. Nardus walked over cautiously and realized that this might turn out to be a turning point. Nardus was never going to go down without a fight, and realizing that he may be heading into one, he was ready to do whatever he needed to do. Even if it meant being killed in the process.

But Nardus was in for a pleasant surprise. Jan was working in the Schouwburg, using his status as a "cooperative Dutchman," only as a means to help do whatever possible to help the knowing and unknowing victims. So instead of a conflict, Nardus had stumbled across an ally and a friend, someone who could help him get word to his comrades outside the Schouwburg.

"Get a message to my sister and brother-in-law," Nardus told Jan. "Tell them that they need to do something to get me out of here as soon as possible. My time is running out."

Two days later, Jan came back to Nardus and gave him a message.

"Jacques Baruch said to me that very soon something will be coming to you, and when you get it, you must use it to get out of there."

Nardus was ready, very ready. He was hungry, thirsty, and tired. His beard was full, and he needed a shower. Since this was war and Holland was under occupation, his condition and appearance was less of a problem than it otherwise normally would have been, but Nardus knew that when he got out, he needed to clean up and get some food, and since in his mind the only options were escaping or dying, he just assumed he was going to get out.

He had designated a relatively quiet spot where Jan could find him if had any news or supplies. That next morning, before the deportation activities had begun, Nardus saw Jan standing in the corner. He motioned him over and handed him a Red Cross arm band.

"Take this, Nardus," he said. "Jacques said to use this and get out of here as soon as you can. However, there is no way you can get out the doors."

"I know this and I have a plan," said Nardus. "Just tell me where the side doors are. Once I get upstairs, I will see if there is a way to the roof."

With a look of exhaustion but powerful determination, Nardus continued, "If I jump off and die, then at least I died trying to be free. I will not stay in here and rot away or be taken away to be murdered. If I make it, then I will go on and help as many people as I can to stay out of this place. And Jan, thank you, and God bless you."

Jan smiled, shook Nardus's hand, and showed him where the doors were that led to the upstairs. The people awaiting transportation would never know this unless they had been frequent concertgoers, and Nardus, because of his somewhat sheltered life in the Jewish ghetto, was not one of those who knew.

The one thing about Nardus was when he would get on the move, the adrenaline would start pumping and he would move without hesitation. He ran up the stairs. And although he had been fatigued by the weeks in putrid conditions, he was a man in very good physical condition. Combine that with the sudden burst of energy he felt by what he saw as his impending freedom, and Nardus was now moving at a furious, albeit controlled, pace.

When he got to the second floor, he saw desks and chairs, but only a few people at work. It was early and the somewhat corrupt and totally misguided administrative staff had not yet completely arrived.

Nardus looked around for his way out. He glanced around the walls, seeing windows, closets, and shelving. All of a sudden, Nardus saw what he knew would be his salvation: a cord to pull down steps to the roof. When he went over, he saw no one was in his line of sight and pulled down the cord. Sure enough, down came the steps that led the roof. With his typical lack of hesitation, Nardus flew up the stairs and, in one quick motion, pulled them up and closed the hatch behind him.

A pain shot into Nardus's eyes. He was outside, in daylight. He had hardly seen daylight in forty days. He put his hands over his eyes and sat down on the roof for what gave him the strength of what felt like a good night's sleep, but in reality was less than one minute.

He got up and went to the edge of the roof; he looked down, sizing up his options. He looked down and the only choice he had, the only chance of surviving, was jumping onto the roof of the neighboring building behind the Schouwburg. It was a long jump down, and Nardus really had no way of knowing what would happen if he jumped; he just knew that he had to, and he knew that he had to without thinking about it. So he jumped.

He landed well. The National Guard training and conditioning had once again paid off. He felt okay. He was now almost completely out of the vision of the Schouwburg, and he knew he was almost there. There were stairs going down the side of the building on which he landed, and just as he needed them to be, they were on the blind side of where he had come from, so once he started down the stairs, he was no longer visible from the Schouwburg.

Now he understood why Jacques had given him the Red Cross armband. He immediately put it on and made it down the stairs. He was almost free.

The stairs ended up in the back yard of a private residence, and now that Nardus was out in the open again, his quick thinking and boldness seemed to return almost immediately.

The only way out was running through the house; Nardus knew that having just escaped Nazi confinement, he was not going to let one simple Dutch family be his demise, so he ran into their house.

The couple sitting in the living room of the house reacted with alarm and anger. The man stood up and shouted at Nardus, "Who are you? What are you doing in our house?"

Without even the slightest bit of hesitation, Nardus pointed to his armband and shouted back, "There's been an accident. I need to go get help."

Whether it was the convincing tone in his voice, the armband, or a lack of will to get into a confrontation, the couple backed down and let Nardus go through their front door, where he found his temporary freedom and safety.

What would always connect Nardus to the Hollandse Schouwburg was that it was unheard of for anyone to escape from being held in confinement in this building. Somehow in later years, in different circles and in different parts of the world, the story of his dramatic escape would become randomly known, even if the name of the person who escaped was not. It never mattered to Nardus. This was not about glory. This was about survival.

FACE TO FACE

With almost everyone now having been taken away, those that remained in Amsterdam were no longer safe anywhere. Many who did manage to flee their homes found refuge in local hiding places or in some of the smaller, more obscure villages in the provinces. Nardus's parents were still in Amsterdam but time was running out for them, as it was for his sister Elizabeth and her husband Aaron. His two older brothers Meyer and David had both managed to secure safe houses, at least for the time being.

As a young adult, Nardus's oldest brother, Meyer, was living in the town of Zutphen in the eastern province of Gelderland. Although the Jewish community of Zutphen was small, the people were close, and everyone got to know each other well. It was there that Meyer met Roe, who became his sweetheart (and later his wife).

In 1942, when the Nazis declared that all Jews needed to be out of the provinces, Meyer and Roe were part of the approximately 50,000 Jews scattered around the country; some of these Jews went to the concentration camps at Westerbork and Vugt. Meyer and Roe went to Amsterdam, and upon their arrival, they found a place to hide in the hope that they could acquire papers allowing them to stay out of any of the camps. Like most of Dutch Jewry, they were not successful in avoiding being captured and were taken to Westerbork. However, at the time they were picked up, as a married couple with the papers they had acquired, rather than being murdered in Westerbork or being sent to a death camp, they ultimately ended up in Theresienstadt, a concentration camp in what is now the Czech Republic.

Despite the image the Nazis tried to create, Theresienstadt was a concentration camp where captives, mainly Jews, were starved, beaten, tortured, and murdered. And even though there were those who made it out alive because of the high profile of the camp, the experience there was another piece of the puzzle that was the devastating experience of Dutch Jewry between 1940 and 1945.

David, the next oldest of Nardus's brothers, also spent time in Westerbork and Theresienstadt, but although there is significant drama, intrigue, and pain in both of their stories, David's story has a special twist to it unlike any other in this entire account.

David, just a few years younger than Meyer, was in hiding with his wife Martha in the home of a non-Jewish family in Amsterdam. David had managed to get word to Nardus of where they were hiding; they were concerned that they were in imminent danger of being picked up. Nardus wanted to see his brother. He knew that he did not have much time left and was not going to wait too much longer to pay him a visit.

Nardus felt that very soon they would all have to leave Amsterdam. Nardus was now living at the *Joodse Invalide,* the Jewish hospital for the handicapped where he had found a temporary bed. It was just a matter of time till the place was raided and gutted. .

So knowing there was very little time left to see his brother, Nardus left the *Joodse Invalide* to go visit David and Martha. Before he left, he went to the storage cabinet and took out a stethoscope. With the curfew being eight o'clock, Nardus intended on passing himself off as a doctor in the event he was confronted by the Green Police.

When he arrived at the house, Nardus saw that the door was open. Something was wrong. He walked up the stairs and found David and Martha, together with the family who lived in the house, standing in front of three members of the Green Police.

Nardus and David were not twins, but there was only a few years age difference between the two, and in their mannerisms and physical appearance, they were very similar. It was not uncommon to have someone mistake one for the other.

David and Nardus made sure not to look at each other, realizing that should they make eye contact, it would only increase the chances that the soldiers would realize they were dealing with two brothers. If this were to happen, Nardus would soon be on his way to Westerbork with the others in the room.

"What are you doing here?" shouted the one officer, looking directly at Nardus's face. "It is almost nine o'clock, and you are out after curfew. What's your story? What are you doing here?"

Seeing that their concern was about the time of day, it was apparent they had not noticed the brothers' resemblance. Nardus was relieved. He now knew that he had a way out. He wanted to help his brother and sister-in-law, but there was nothing he could do right now. Anything he would say or do would only lead to him being taken away as well. He reached into his pocket and took out the stethoscope.

"I'm a doctor," he told the soldier. Looking toward Martha, he continued, "I am here to examine these people and see if they need any medical treatment."

The soldiers had no interest in the health of the people they were about to ship out to a concentration camp; they wasted no time making sure this man they now believed was a doctor was made very aware of that.

"Get out of here!" the soldier shouted at Nardus. "She doesn't need your care anymore. Go home. And don't come out after curfew again."

Nardus was happy to oblige. He knew he had narrowly escaped capture. He turned around to leave, giving a quick glance over to his brother who was not as fortunate and was on his way to Westerbork with his wife. He could only pray that he would see them again.

SURGICAL CONSEQUENCES

As fate would have it, the person that all the evidence pointed to as being responsible for David and Martha's arrest as well as another narrow escape for Nardus took ill less than a week after this took place The events that took place would not be privy to Nardus till much later, but what appeared to happen was that the said individual suffered some sort of internal, abdominal emergency.

When word got out what had happened, the right people were ready. The doctor in the hospital was working together with the Resistance and would have the assistance of certain underground activists when the time came to work on the man they now had evidence of being the traitor.

Even the most equipped of the hospitals had a makeshift feeling to them these days. Doctors and nurses were either very hard to find or were working with so few supplies that they were often incapable of performing their functions at a high level. To make matters worse, the controls being used to monitor other activities and movements were focused on other areas. There just wasn't any priority being put on the medical care of the average Dutch citizen. The Nazis were not killing Dutch people en masse, but they also had no intention of going out of their way to see to it that they remained in good health either.

So on any given day, the activities in a hospital could be performed with an accidental (or in this particular case, purposeful) recklessness.

The doctor performing the surgery waited for the anesthesia to kick in, made the initial incision, and proceeded to turn to the only nurse present, a middle-aged Dutch woman oblivious to what was really taking place, and gave her a specific instruction. He made sure to request something he knew was not in the room; she would be gone for at least two minutes. That was all he would need. There were two other men with him, both from the Resistance, and they just stood there quietly listening and observing, not revealing the firearms at their sides they had prepared should anything go wrong.

The nurse paused.

"It's okay," said the doctor. "I have it under control. I'll keep an eye on him and wait to do anything else until you return."

The nurse looked at the doctor and then at the two other men; her face looked more relaxed now. She nodded in agreement and walked out the door.

As soon as the door closed, one of the men reached into his pocket and pulled out a syringe. He handed it to the doctor, who in turn quickly injected it into the patient's arm. The drug would take about five minutes to take effect, at which time the man would go into cardiac arrest.

The nurse returned and they continued with the surgery. A few minutes later, the drug took effect.

From the perspective of the Resistance, the surgery was a success. The patient never woke up. He died on the operating table in what was the only way of administering justice in these lawless times.

THEA

Most of the people sent to Westerbork were only there for a short period of time. Most of the Jews to go through the camp would go on to the death camps of Auschwitz or Sobibor. There was, however, a small population of permanent residents of the camp. These were mainly married couples; many would eventually be sent to Theresienstadt, as was the case with Nardus's brother and sister-in-law, Meyer and Roe.

Upon their seizure in Amsterdam, David and Martha Groen were sent to Westerbork as well. Even though they had Jewish parents, they also had baptismal papers in hand, so the Nazis decided for now that they could live as part of the permanent population. This allowed them to actually live as husband and wife, albeit in what were less than positive conditions. However, what was to happen as a result was as unprecedented as any other during the years of the Nazi occupation of Holland.

Martha was pregnant. And once again, because of the paperwork indicating they were baptized (something they had Jacques Baruch to thank for), Martha was allowed to carry the baby to term and deliver the baby in Westerbork. On January 1, 1944, David and Martha Groen became the proud parents of a beautiful baby girl, who they would name Thea.

The first amazing factor in the young girl's birth was, of course, the fact that it took place in a concentration camp. For this to happen was so rare that it is difficult to find actual documentation of children born in camps at all. That in itself made her birth remarkable. What made it even more remarkable was the fact that with the natural beauty of Martha and the fair complexion of David, the baby was so fair skinned and blonde that the Germans saw her as a beautiful Aryan child. This in turn would, at least for now, save her life as well as the life of her parents.

After the baby was born, David, Martha, and Thea were sent to Theresienstadt, the "model camp."

In the eyes of the Nazis, the three of them were perfect for this camp. They were a young couple, with a beautiful baby, showing the world that the conditions in the camps were not as bad as everyone was making them out to be. That, more than anything, was the purpose of Theresienstadt: to create this false image of decency and morality within the concentration camps, when in truth, millions had already been killed and many more would not only be killed in the other camps, but in Theresienstadt as well.

The Germans would take the game one step further, and David, Martha, and Thea would have no choice but to be pawns in their game. The young attractive couple with the stunningly beautiful young baby would be sent to Switzerland, where the Red Cross would see them, examine them, and find them to be healthy and strong. David and Martha knew what was going on, they knew they were being used, but they also knew that nothing they would say or do to dispute the image being portrayed would change anything that was happening in Theresienstadt, Westerbork, or any of the death camps in other parts of Europe. The only thing they would have done is sign their own death warrants, leaving Thea to most likely either be killed or raised by a Nazi official or collaborator. So they played the game that needed to be played and allowed themselves to be displayed for the Red Cross.

Had the war continued for longer than it had, the chances of David and Martha being allowed to live would have decreased significantly. But when the Red Cross took over Theresienstadt on May 1, 1945, followed a week later by the liberation of the camp by Soviet troops, David and Martha were still alive. They didn't know yet what they would do or where they would go, but they did know that had it not been for their beautiful little girl, Thea, the chances that they would have been alive to build a life would have been slim at best. If ever a baby was a blessing to parents, Thea Groen was a blessing to hers.

In what was an era of killing and suffering, where entire generations of people were being wiped out, and where families' histories and legacies were being destroyed, Thea Groen was the one representation of hope, joy, but most of all life. And for a family whose future was very much in question, she was the first of what would hopefully be a new generation.

A DAY OF DEATH AND DESPAIR

If you've ever been to Holland for any extended period of time, you know that it is not known for having pleasant weather. It's been calculated that at least two thirds of the year is either very damp or rainy. If it's not the type of environment you are used to, it more than likely will feel somewhat gloomy and maybe even depressing. For the Dutch, it's just normal. It's the way it is. Wet weather is to be expected; it creates no feeling of gloom or doom. However, on the night of July 14, 1942, the pervading feeling of gloom was so strong it made the rain feel like pellets of fire against Nardus's face. He knew what was going on. He saw it developing and he just knew. No one in Holland had any idea of the details of the horrors taking place, but throughout Europe, Jews were being rounded up and shipped away to obscure locations, never to return. The Nazis made no secret of their disdain for Jews, but until now they had done a good job of masking their intentions. It had not been spoken or announced, but this day was the beginning stage of their master plan, which was to make sure that no Jews were left alive in Amsterdam.

Nardus did not know where the Jews were going or what exactly was happening to them, but the one thing he did know was that it was treacherous at best and horrific at worst. The advantage he had over many other friends and colleagues was that instead of having what was considered a Jew face (*Joden koop*), Nardus looked like a rather typical Dutchman. This was a trait that he was now to going to use to his benefit. Now that the Germans had begun to remove Jews from their homes, it was time for

Nardus to leave his neighborhood and become part of the Resistance. His activities were designed to hopefully make two things occur: he would survive, and he would assist in the survival of as many other people as possible, starting of course with his family and closest friends.

For Sipora, July 14, 1942, was a day that would change her life forever. She was already living out of the house and studying and working in the hospital. She had no way of knowing at first which people close to her were victims of this raid that had taken place, but with the large numbers taken from their homes, she knew that bad news was coming. And that it did. On July 14, 1942, her fiancé Hans was taken from his home, later to be killed.

Hans de Jong: Murdered August 13, 1942, Auschwitz.

THEY MEET

Sipora had decided at a relatively young age that she would become a registered nurse. It was perfect for her. She had already had a position of responsibility in her own home, and in many ways, moving on to a position that involved caring for other people was a natural progression in her life.

According to Dutch law, one cannot begin practicing as a nurse until the age of twenty, so it was not until 1942 that Sipora would begin her employment at the Nederlandse Israelitsche Ziekenhous (NIZ, which translated into English means "Dutch Israeli Hospital"). She had studied to be a nurse and wanted to be one for a long time, but it was not until after Hans was taken away that she actually made the move and began working. Many of the Jews of Amsterdam had no home left to go to, and for Sipora, this was no different. The only place that held any meaning for her at this point was the NIZ.

This of course was not the way she had pictured the way her life would go. Her mother had died seven years earlier, her father and brother were in danger every day, and her fiancé Hans had been seized and transported away by the Nazis, with little hope of ever returning.

Sipora felt very alone, and the hospital was where she found the closest thing to solace. It was where she lived, where she ate, and of course where she worked. For someone who had no one left and really nowhere to go, you can say that her job was what kept her alive. It was the only thing that would give her some reason to even begin her day.

Her days were never easy ones. Even if the war had not begun and the Nazis had not occupied Holland, this was still a time of economic hardship throughout Europe. People were struggling to survive financially, and illness was more common than it had been in previous years. The job of a registered nurse, not easy in any time, was even more difficult in this time. In some ways, this was a good thing for Sipora, because it kept her busy and her mind occupied, but at the end of the day, or during break times in the middle of the day, she needed a distraction. That distraction was to be found in the game room.

Sipora as a nurse in NIZ

The game room was where hospital employees and visitors would go to relax, chat, have a cup of tea or coffee, and let off some steam. There were many men who would come to the hospital, whether it was to volunteer, to work, or just to find people from similar backgrounds to connect with. Many of them would just come for a good game of ping-pong. They were not all employees of the hospital, and frankly Sipora did not even know who many of them were. This was unimportant to her, since the games were fun to watch and a nice relaxing distraction from the hardships and realities of her life.

One of the young men who came to play was a slender redhead with deep blue eyes. He was one of the best of all the players. And when he picked up the ping-pong paddle, he was fun to watch; Sipora enjoyed watching him immensely. She hardly noticed what he actually looked like because she had no romantic interest in him, but when he played, it was a pleasure to watch. The loss of Hans was still fresh, and the last thing on her mind was becoming involved with someone else. Sipora's priority was just getting through the day.

Sipora found herself becoming more and more interested in the ping-pong games. She had not played it much herself and was so impressed by the skill and speed involved. And most importantly, when she was there in the game room, watching the young men playing ping-pong, the harsh realities of the world she was now living in were outside the door, and she was able, at least to some extent, to have some slight degree of a good time.

More and more, as she watched these games, she noticed the young man with the red hair and blue eyes. She did not know him at all and figured by his appearance that he was more than likely not Jewish. He had an intelligent, sympathetic look about him and was clearly very respectful to the people he came in contact with. But for Sipora, most of all, it was fun watching him play ping-pong. However, she also began to notice that his eyes would more and more often be directed her way when they were not focused on the ping-pong table.

Like any young woman, Sipora was beginning to enjoy the attention, even if only a little. At a time when she had no one, the fact that someone was specifically paying attention to her made her feel slightly less alone.

This was good. In times like these, it was the type of thing that would keep someone going.

Although she had been forced to reach a certain maturity as an adult at a young age, Sipora was in many ways very innocent. The only man she had ever perceived in any romantic way had been Hans, and even that was kept somewhat distant in her thoughts; they had waited to be intimate until their wedding. So Nardus Groen, this man with the red hair and blue eyes, this man whose skill at ping-pong truly fascinated her, was a man she perceived as nothing more than a friend. In fact, the first words they spoke to each other were not about the war, nor the Nazi occupation, nor the Jewish community that was being rampaged. These words certainly did not portend any inkling toward any romantic involvement. Only one thing was to draw them together in the very beginning. And that was ping-pong.

"I see you are very good at this game," Sipora said to Nardus as she watched him play one evening. "Is it possible to learn how to play? It looks like it is very difficult."

"Well, it's like anything else," he replied. "It's easy once you know how. My name is Nardus. Would you like me to teach you how to play?"

Sipora was not sure what was more exciting to her: the fact that she might learn how to play this game or the fact that she now had someone to talk to, maybe a new friend. Either way, the answer was an easy one.

"Oh, would you?" she replied. "I would like very much to learn how to play. I watch the games whenever I get a chance, and it seems like a lot of fun. Thank you so much. My name is Sippy. Very nice to meet you."

From this point on, Nardus and Sipora got to know each other. She learned a little bit about the game of ping-pong, probably not as much as she had originally anticipated; they talked of their neighborhoods and history, and discussed the state of affairs as they knew them to be in Amsterdam.

Nardus was staying in the nearby Joodse Invalide and found his way over to the NIZ on a more and more regular basis.

Sipora eventually learned that this man, who she had originally pegged as not being Jewish, was indeed not only Jewish but actually had grown up a strictly practicing Jew in the ghetto of Amsterdam. This too was cause for some fascination on Sipora's part, because although she was not from a religious background, the Jews of Amsterdam were not that detached from each other. Sipora's family belonged to the Esnoga, the synagogue Nardus occasionally visited back in better, freer times.

As the time went on and they got to know each other better, Nardus developed a much stronger romantic interest toward Sipora than she had toward him. Although she was enjoying his friendship, the real difference was due to Sipora's frame of mind. She had reached the point where she was emotionally cold and closed off. She was only interested in whatever would get her through the day, and any thoughts of the future were beyond her abilities. This didn't mean she wasn't getting closer to Nardus, though. She was developing a trust toward him that she needed in order to deal with the horrors they were being more frequently exposed to.

Raids on Jewish homes, people being shipped out of the city, being treated like animals wherever the Nazis took them. Most notable of all these locations was the Hollandse Schouwburg, the former concert hall. Sipora had frequented the Schouwburg in her earlier years, and when she heard that it had been transformed into a place where Jews were being processed before being transported to concentration camps, it was just one more example that her world was slipping away. Nardus's company, his mere presence, was in some ways the only good thing she had at this time. If nothing else, she appreciated the support she felt when he was around.

Nardus was cut from a different cloth. He was less emotional, more in control of his situation. Part of it had to do with his physical appearance. While someone like Sipora, with darker skin and dark hair, was always concerned with being identified as a Jew by the Nazis, a fair-haired, light-skinned man such as Nardus could walk the streets of Amsterdam without having to be concerned that German soldiers or Dutch collaborators would identify him and turn him as a Jew.

He had seen some horrors himself by this time, but his clarity of the situation, which allowed him to grasp the realities of what was happening, as well as his strong fighting nature, kept him moving forward without needing anyone else to lean on. So although his romantic interest in Sipora was greater, he did not turn to her out of a need for security or support. Truth be told, he just liked her from the beginning. Although her feelings were not of the romantic nature like his were, she would end up needing him, at least at this stage, far more than he would need her.

The one fact they both shared was that for both of them, getting to know each other well in these horrific times was something positive. It would give both of them, especially Sipora, some remnant of hope.

AARON AND ELIZABETH

With the raids increasing in frequency, the population of Nardus's neighborhood was diminishing in size with startling regularity and consistency. He and Jacques, together with other members of the growing underground Resistance, were doing all they could to help people either get out or at the very least delay or diminish their perils.

Jacques played the greatest role within Nardus's close circles in the provision of false papers. These papers indicated that the person in question had been baptized and was no longer a practicing member of the Jewish faith. Jacques was able to get papers to Nardus's brother Meyer and his wife Roe, and his brother David and his wife Martha. He also had papers for himself and his wife, Nardus's sister Sofia, and one for Nardus himself.

While Jacques was trying to secure papers for his sister-in-law, Elizabeth Groen, and her fiancé Aaron Mozes, he had managed to acquire papers for Leendert and Marjan Groen. They refused to accept them, being that it required them to, at least in public, denounce their belief in Judaism and the Jewish way of life. With Elizabeth living at home with her parents, Jacques was hopeful that through Aaron Mozes, he might have a chance of saving his young sister-in-law.

Aaron's mental state never recovered after he was released from Amersfoort, making it back to where it had been a few years back; this made the acquisition of acceptable papers as well as his cooperation far more difficult. Elizabeth loved Aaron and would not leave his side, but she knew that the man she loved today was not the man she had fallen in love with a few years back. The time he had spent in Amersfoort had taken such a toll on his emotional and physical state, that even once Jacques acquired the correct papers, his safety would be far from guaranteed. His weakened condition put him in danger regardless of what paperwork he was carrying.

Despite all of this, Elizabeth's love for Aaron was unwavering. She would stay with him and hope that the world as it was unfolding before them would allow them some sort of life together. One thing she did know for certain: Whether she was with Aaron or not, neither she nor anyone else around her was safe. If the dangers existed anyway, she might as well bring some joy into their lives, no matter how short lived that joy would be.

On September 28, 1942, Elizabeth met with Aaron at his parents' to discuss their plans. After speaking with his parents, Elizabeth planned to talk with hers. Had these been normal times, Aaron would have been there with her, but it was getting later in the day and being outside past midday was becoming more and more of an unnecessary risk to take.

Feeling a comfort and happiness in her decision didn't take away the nervousness Elizabeth felt as she walked into the living room to sit and talk with her parents. She was a twenty-one-year-old woman, yet she was still their little girl, and living at home; whatever she would do in her life would, as a matter of respect, require her parents' knowledge and approval. Elizabeth knew what she wanted to do, and with Leendert and Marjan Groen being Jewish parents with old-fashioned values, she knew she required their blessing.

When she walked in, her father was sitting and reading, as her mother sat with a cup of hot tea.

"Papi and Mami," she said in a tired, yet determined voice, "I need to speak with you about something very important."

Seeing the seriousness in his daughter's eyes, Leendert answered immediately. "What is wrong, my child?"

"I want to marry Aaron," she said, getting straight to the point. Knowing that her parents already knew that the two had been planning to marry, Elizabeth continued without pause, making the point she really needed to make. "I, we, want to do it tomorrow. Every day more people are being taken away, to God knows where, and I may not ever get the chance to be Mrs. Aaron Mozes if I do not do this soon."

Leendert looked over at his wife. She was not a woman to be expressive with her emotions and would, on most occasions, defer to Leendert to make the statements of affection toward their children. She was a loving and caring mother, but her personality was one that did not normally allow her to show emotion. Today would be one of those exceptions. She and Leendert looked at each other, communicating to each other an understanding of all that was going on and may continue to go on. Knowing that her husband felt just as she did, Marjan spoke for both of them as she said, "It will be our joy to see you marry Aaron. Both your father and I give you our blessing and look forward to tomorrow."

Leendert sat back smiling as he saw his daughter's eyes light up.

"I'll speak to the rabbi," he said. "We can do this early tomorrow morning. He will find the way to get this done, I am sure."

Elizabeth hugged them both, laughing and crying at the same time. She would be a bride in what was a very sad time. She left her parents in the living room and went to put together the best outfit she could find.

In the living room, without saying a word to each other, Leendert and Marjan looked into each other's eyes once again. Leendert saw the joy in his wife's eyes turn to sadness. She then looked away from him and dropped her head, praying to herself that her daughter and soon-to-be son-in-law would have an opportunity to enjoy their lives together.

As he had promised his daughter, Leendert Groen made all the necessary arrangements for his daughter's wedding the following morning. The ceremony was held in a shop, formerly owned by one of their friends and now being run by a former employee who was decent and sympathetic to the plight of the Jewish community. Everyone moved toward the back, where they would not be visible from the street. The ceremony met all the requirements of Jewish law, which included four men, each holding a corner of a prayer shawl over the heads of the bride and groom, creating the traditional "*Chupah*" or wedding canopy. The service was brief but joyful. As Aaron stepped on the glass cup, shattering it into pieces, signifying the last component of the ceremony, whatever family and friends that had been able to be present let out a roar of "*Mazal Tov!*" ("Congratulations").

Times being as they were, the opportunity to celebrate beyond this point just did not exist. Aaron and Elizabeth didn't care. They were now married and could at least hope to live their days together as a couple.

With the Green Police patrolling the neighborhood, not only was it not safe for Jews to stay out on the street for a long time, it was also not advisable for them to congregate for any significant length of time. So when the family and wedding guests left the shop, they decided to do so in incremental fashion. Marjan and Leendert left first, followed by most of their family and many of Aaron's family. When they arrived home, just three blocks away, they heard what were now the familiar and ominous sounds of Nazi vehicles driving through the area. They heard the cars and trucks stopping and soldiers shouting; another raid had begun.

The feeling of helplessness on this day for Leendert and Marjan Groen was immeasurable. Their youngest daughter, their little girl, had just gotten married, not even an hour earlier, and now all they could do was wait. Wait and sit, and pray, that she and Aaron would be safe and that they would see them again.

Two hours later, Jacques Baruch walked through the doorway of Leendert and Marjan Groen's house. Leendert stood and approached him as Marjan looked on, not moving from her spot. The expression on Jacques's face told them the news they were so terrified to hear, but as of yet had not confirmed.

Jacques shook his head slowly from side to side, the anguish evident in his face.

Leendert opened his mouth and in saying the two names, formed the question all three in the room knew needed to be asked.

"Elizabeth and Aaron?" The names came off his lips, the dread evident in his tone.

Jacques put his head down, not able to look at his in-laws' faces, and just said, "They're gone."

There was no stopping in Westerbork for Aaron and Elizabeth Mozes. The trip to the death camp was direct and the newlyweds became two of the latest victims of the Nazi killing machine. They both perished in Auschwitz.

Aaron and Elizabeth Mozes
Married: Amsterdam, September 28, 1942
Picked up by the SS, September 28, 1942
Murdered: - September 30, 1942,- Auschwitz

RIGHTEOUS MARTYRDOM

Entering into February of 1943, Leendert and Marjan Groen were still in Amsterdam. They knew, however, that it was just a matter of time until the Germans came for them, and nothing could prevent it. Nardus's parents were among those not willing to allow the Nazi war machine to dictate their actions. They did need to do something, however. The Jews of Amsterdam were being systematically rounded up and shipped to concentration camps. There were many fake identification passes being produced by the underground resources in Amsterdam, and Jacques Baruch had managed to acquire two passes for Leendert and Marjan. Nardus's parents also had the advantage of not looking as Jewish as many others did, so with the passes and a little bit of good fortune, their chances of survival would at least increase somewhat with the false papers. The one thing they needed to do, however, the most important thing, was to live, to act, and to pretend to not be Jewish.

Jacques recalled the time he had first approached Leendert to tell him what he felt was relatively good news.

"I have managed to acquire the means in which you may get through this situation safely," he told him. Jacques went on to say, "These passes will allow you to stay in Amsterdam, and more than likely no one will bother you. The names on the passes need to be your new names for as long as the Nazis control the city. You need to find a place to live, but as long as no one knows you are Jewish, you have a far better chance of making it through. The main thing is that you will be safe."

Leendert Groen was a mild-mannered, humble, and pleasant man; he was also a man of great conviction and great faith. The one thing in life that for him was always stable, consistent, and real was his faith. He knew what this meant. He understood that it meant not only not being able to live as a Jew, it also meant that he had to deny the very fact that he was a Jew.

He looked at Jacques with a warm smile and stated very clearly, "I was born as a Jew, and I will die as a Jew. If we are able to survive what is to come, we will not do so pretending to be anything other than what we are."

Marjan, the pillar of strength and character that she was, would not challenge this in any way, shape, or form. She too believed that the life they were leading was the correct life, and that if God wanted them to survive, they would survive as Jews.

Leendert took the fake identification cards, handed them to Jacques, and said, "I am truly grateful for what you are trying to do, I truly am, and I know that there will be people who will make the choice to go the direction you are suggesting. We, however, will not. I will not stop living as a Jew for anyone. Even if it means I die sooner as a result."

The raid that took place on February 1, 1943, cleared out most of what was left of Nardus's neighborhood. He went to the neighborhood and saw the darkness and felt the emptiness. Everyone was gone. Everything he knew had changed and would never again be as he remembered it. He was now officially on the run and would remain this way until the war was over.

As the last remaining Jews of Amsterdam were being forcibly loaded on a train, Leendert and Marjan Groen looked to fulfill just one wish before they were taken away. Leendert looked for the one person he needed to see before they left. And that person was Jacque Baruch.

When he found him, he had but one sentence for him:

"Please look after my family and make sure they are safe and taken care of." These were the last words that anyone close to Leendert Groen ever heard.

Leendert and Marjan Groen: Murdered February 5, 1943, Auschwitz.

CONFRONTING THE DEVIL

The process of raiding public institutions and facilities was one the Nazis had mastered for quite a while now. It began with the transportation of the weakest and ended with the rounding up of whatever management would remain to hold the fort. In the case of the hospital, their methods were even more pronounced and obvious. The sickest and most elderly of the patients were the first to be taken away, while the doctors, nurses, and administrative staff remained behind to care for the remaining patients and maintain the appearance of a functioning institution.

Sipora watched in anguish as more and more people were taken away. None of this was done with any compassion or anything that resembled care for the condition of the patients. It was clear that these people were not being taken away for their benefit. Elderly, sick, and frail people were being rounded up and loaded onto transports with no regard for their respect or dignity.

The raids began somewhere around November of 1942. As they became more frequent, the behavior of the Nazis became more efficient and more precise. The closer they came to completing the process of emptying out the hospital, the more often the higher ranking officers would appear. The raids generally took place on Fridays, as means of showing contempt toward the start of the Jewish Sabbath.

The raids were done entirely at random. This was part of the plan. The people would know the raids were coming, they just wouldn't know when, adding to the terror surrounding each raid. For the Nazis, no raid was different from another, other than the fact that each time they raided the hospital, they managed to decrease the number of patients remaining.

Everything was going exactly as they had planned. They were eliminating the Jews from these locations in incremental fashion, just as they had been instructed. What had once been a full facility had now dwindled down to between one-quarter and one-half full.

One Friday night was a special one for the SS officers in charge of emptying out the hospital. What made that raid special was that the main SS administrator, Ferdinand Aus der Funten himself, made an appearance to see firsthand the progress his soldiers had made.

The entire remaining staff was ordered to come to the main lobby. The officer in charge wanted to put on a show for his boss, and having the administration there to watch would be a humiliation he knew would impress him. The intention of the raids was not only to diminish the Jewish population of Amsterdam but also to crush the spirit of those who remained. By making the remaining hospital staff witness the removal of these patients, it would remove any thought of resistance or any hope for a bright future.

Aus der Funten appeared pleased. His staff had done an excellent job of combining a degree of subtlety with the horror taking place. Any patient able to walk was being forced to do so, while a number were in wheelchairs, with only those totally incapacitated taken out on stretchers. Most of the ill were crying or moaning, feeling the excessive force with which they were being removed, while some were literally crying out in pain.

As pleased as he appeared with his people's efforts, Aus der Funten also seemed gratified when his men wheeled out the last of the patients chosen for the night's deportation. Sipora watched the look on this man's face as the sick were being forcibly removed in front of him. She watched with utter distaste the treatment and behavior of this man who was responsible, at least on the local level, for what was taking place. His face was void of compassion and permeated arrogance. She did not know him personally, but looking at him, she already hated him.

Some people at least appeared to become more and more immune to what they were witnessing with each passing raid, but Sipora was not one of them. Not knowing the extent of the Nazis' intentions and having been brought up in an environment where such behavior was abhorrent, Sipora could not keep quiet much longer. And as a nurse in the hospital, she felt that she had every right to speak up.

With the raid completed, Aus der Funten took one final stroll around the lobby of the hospital. He inspected his soldiers and passed by the hospital staff with an air of domineering scorn. Too caught up in the brutality and tragedy of the situation, Sipora's fear dissipated and was replaced with a rage she had never felt before. She glared at Aus der Funten and shouted, "Why are you doing this?"

In the unscrupulous manner he had done everything else to this point, he looked away from Sipora and the remaining staff and with scorn in his voice responded, *"Das mutte der rabijnen vragen,"* meaning, "Go ask your rabbis."

He turned to his men and said, "Let's get out of this shithole." They turned and left, leaving the hospital closer to a complete state of ruin. Sipora hung her head and began to cry.

Certificate allowing Sipora to work as a Jewish nurse and have at least temporary exemption from arrest or deportation. It is signed by Aus der Funten

SCARLET FEVER

With the raids increasing in frequency, it was only a matter of time before the Nazis would look to remove the staff from the hospital as well. With each passing raid, the nurses, Sipora included, were becoming more and more fearful for their safety. After her outburst directed at Aus der Funten, Sipora knew that the officers who witnessed it would love to get their hands on her. So besides the obvious concerns surrounding her appearance, she had to hope they didn't get too many good looks at her as well.

With the nurses' complex attached to the main hospital, the resident staff was able to hide away somewhat separate from where the main activities were taking place. Unless they were looking for nurses in particular, keeping a distance meant they were able to avoid the Nazi rampages taking place. In hearing the arrival of the buses, the nurses would go straight to the room they had arranged to congregate in and just wait. When the raid was over, Nardus or one of the other underground activists living in the institution would come and let them know it was safe to return.

One day, the raid seemed even more unscrupulous. Even with the distance between the main hospital and the nurses' quarters, they still could hear the sounds of the terror taking place.

The nurses, always looking for ways to stay busy, came up with various games and competitions amongst themselves. It seemed almost amoral to be having any sort of fun while right outside their door, people were being picked up to be taken to their death, but the purpose was not trivial amusement. They needed to keep busy to keep their sanity. And their sanity translated to better treatment and conditions for those patients left behind. With their self-imposed isolation lasting an undetermined amount of time, they needed to keep active somehow.

On this day, the nurses needed a greater mental diversion than usual. So the game was to see who had the largest breasts. For these young women, in a time when modesty had a different definition than it does in the twenty-first century, this was a rather risqué adventure. But that was the idea. The greater the need for distraction, the greater the need for something outrageous.

Nardus had been visiting Sipora when the raid started. Knowing that the nurses were in their room and helpless should the Nazis look to transport them, he waited near the door, standing guard. There would be no physical means of stopping them should they decide to smash through the door and take them, so he had come up with an approach that might work. Nardus wasn't so naïve to think that one young Dutchman in front of a room full of nurses could tell a band of Green Police and SS storm troopers what to do, but appearing to look out for their health and well-being might go over with far better results. Should they come for the nurses, he knew what he was going to do.

Nardus stood there and heard the giggles coming from the room behind him. Although he did not have the luxury of even cracking a smile with the enemy no more than seconds away, it was good to know that the nurses were able to enjoy each other's company. Prior to them closing the door, he told them to listen for one tap on the door. Between that and the need to hear the soldiers approaching from inside the room, the nurses toned down the sounds of their activities.

When the sounds of soldiers approaching grew louder, Nardus gave the door one quick tap. The laughter and conversation stopped. A group of five or six soldiers entered the main lobby where he was standing. When they saw him, two or three of the soldiers came right over to him while the rest smashed in doors, their rifles cocked, looking for others that might be hiding.

The senior officer that had approached him spoke first.

"Get out of the way. We need to see if anyone is in that room," he commanded.

In a cooperative and noncombative tone, Nardus answered, "I will do what you say, but you should know the room is a quarantined area of patients with scarlet fever. Anyone going in there does so at their own risk."

The soldiers began to talk amongst themselves in German. They seemed uncomfortable and agitated. His plan appeared to be working.

"It's ugly in there," continued Nardus. "The rashes and scabs are spreading; many of the patients are having trouble breathing."

"You've been in there?" asked the Nazi officer.

"I had no choice," replied Nardus. "Someone has to attend to them. For me to stay here, I had to do the job they gave me."

The Germans were terrified of scarlet fever. Between the rashes and sores on different parts of the body, and the painful and often permanent damage to internal organs, these soldiers wanted no part of anything that would bring them close to any type of exposure. In their eyes, this now included Nardus.

The senior officer said something to the others as they all backed up, looking at Nardus.

"Have fun," he said to Nardus with sarcastic contempt. "We're not touching you or those diseases in there."

They turned and marched out the way they had come in. Minutes later, the trucks pulled away, leaving no more than a handful of patients and the nurses in the room right behind Nardus.

OUT THE WINDOW AND ON THE MOVE

The date was Friday, August 13, 1943, and it felt like the worst moment of Sipora's young life. She knew that the Germans were in the building and getting closer to finding her. She had already been through so much and she knew that the situation was going to get a lot worse before it got better. Her will to live was being taken over by despair. She was not the type of woman who would do anything to speed up her own death, but she also did not feel like running or fighting. So she decided that she would just wait on the third floor, and when the Nazi soldiers located her, she would willingly leave together with the rest of the patients and hospital staff. At least then she felt as though she could do some good by making the sick and elderly patients a little more comfortable.

Nardus, however, had no intention of allowing this to happen. As had been the case since the beginning of the Nazi invasion of Amsterdam, he instinctively knew that whatever Jews were not murdered instantly would instead suffer greatly through torture, experimentation, rape, or brutal slave labor. Since he found Sipora before the soldiers did, he knew he had to get her out. And to a man like Nardus, it did not matter what Sipora thought of this idea. It was going to happen his way. And that was that.

When Sipora saw Nardus, she had already sunk so deep into hopelessness she wasn't able to feel any sense of relief. And she was determined to let him know.

"I am just going to wait here and let them take me too," she told Nardus. "They will need a nurse for the trip. If nothing else I can make the others feel more comfortable."

Some moments define an individual, and other moments can define a relationship between two individuals. In many ways, what was about to take place would define much of Nardus and Sipora's relationship. True to his nature, Nardus was not suggesting or asking what would happen next. What he was doing was telling Sipora what would happen next.

"I'll tell you what," he said in his straight-to-the-point manner, "since you are going to your death anyway, and that is your plan, I will throw you out the window right now myself. At least then you will die quickly. Either way you will die."

Sipora began crying. "What's the point?" she said. "There's no hope. My family is gone, your family is gone. They're even taking sick and old patients from here and transporting them out of the city."

Knowing that he needed to remain calm and in control, Nardus made it very clear to Sipora what was to happen next.

"Get up and let's get out of here. We will find a way to survive this. All you have to do is trust me and listen to what I tell you to do."

Although what she was experiencing felt like hell, Sipora was at least able to move now. What made the difference was that someone else, someone she was growing to trust more and more by the day, was taking control and leading her in what at least felt like a better direction.

Neither Nardus nor Sipora had any idea what was to come next, but it did not matter. The only thing that mattered now was that Nardus would never allow either one of them to just sit and wait to be killed.

At this moment, which signified all the drama, horror, and significance of the times they were living through, these two people were thrust together in a way that set the tone for all that was yet to come.

NIZ (Nederlandse Israelitsche Ziekenhous)

Nardus knew that there was little time to waste. But he had a plan. The *Joodse Invalide* was not far, and after the final raid by the Nazis in the beginning of March, there was minimal traffic in and out of the building. It would not be safe for long, but it would be safe for now, and that was all he was concerned with. He looked out the window. This appeared to be the final raid that would take place in this hospital, so whatever he did, he needed to do with speed and accuracy. He was going to get Sipora out of here alive and then he would stay with her until he could find her some other location not under constant threat of a Nazi raid.

His next move was clear cut. He needed to get back to Sipora and get them out of there.

Sipora waited in her room. The noises from outside were horrific. The sounds of German soldiers shouting, patients crying, and dogs barking kept repeating itself. Nardus had been gone for only a few minutes and yet it seemed like a lifetime. When the door opened and he stood there before her, alert and determined, the noises from the outside went away for a few moments. She needed the strength to move, the strength to follow him.

And what gave her this strength was the feeling of hope his behavior had inspired in her. For those few yet unforgettable moments, Sipora traveled to a better place and time, allowing her mind to drift away and dream. Dream of a future. Dream of living. It was Nardus's voice that would startle her back to reality.

"We have to move now," he told her with ice in his voice. "We only have a few minutes to get to the lobby. If we are not at the front door soon, they will figure out that something is amiss. We need to get you out as a patient. Follow me."

Sipora took Nardus's hand as they moved with quiet haste down the corner staircase. The set of stairs they were taking would lead them into the furthest corner of the patients' quarters. There Nardus could find a gurney to place Sipora on and wheel her out of the building.

Nardus opened the door into the ward with caution, ever mindful that they were running out of time.

"Over there," he motioned to Sipora. Ten feet from where they stood were two stretchers. "Lie down and don't speak. Remember, you are supposed to be ill, so it's okay if you make sounds. Just do not speak until I say."

Sipora lay down on the stretcher, and Nardus covered her face and body with a sheet. Not lost on Sipora was the gentle care he took when pulling it over her face. Sipora was ready. She closed her eyes and waited for the stretcher to move. Now everything was up to Nardus. Her life was in his hands.

Nardus was not quite ready yet. He needed two more things. First, he needed a surgical mask. Right there in front of him was the closet. He opened it and saw a bag of them. He put one on his face, covering his mouth and nose, and another he put in his pocket. Almost ready, he needed just one more thing. He looked around for a few seconds. There it was. He found what he was looking for. He walked over to the table, picked up a large scalpel, and carefully put it in his pocket. He had all he needed for now. He and Sipora were now ready to head for the front door.

"This woman is very ill," he told the Nazi officers as they arrived at the main doorway of the hospital. "Do not come too close. She is contagious."

The Nazi soldiers backed up and pointed to a bus outside.

"Go to that bus over there. It's got all the nurses. Let them deal with this shit."

Nardus got Sipora on one of the buses specifically designated to transport people over to the Joodse Invalide and took a quick look around. There were definitely some on this bus who were mobile enough to get out and find members of the resistance should they choose to do so. Maybe this would give them a better chance of survival. There was no way of ever knowing for sure, but if they wished to get off the bus and make that attempt, Nardus was going to see to it that they would get that opportunity.

He walked to the front and told the bus driver to stop after the next turn. The driver was a Dutchmen, but he showed reluctance and some fear when he replied to Nardus.

"It's too dangerous," he said, trying to sound somewhat commanding. "I was instructed to take these people to the Joodse Invalide."

Nardus reached into his pocket and pulled out the scalpel he had taken before they had left the N.I.Z. After he was sure the driver was able to see what he was holding in his hand Nardus spoke to the driver in a calm voice.

"They did not count how many people got on this bus and let me be very clear", Nardus said coldly. "It will be more dangerous if you do not stop."

The bus turned the corner and pulled over, allowing a number of people to get out in the hope that they would find their way to freedom. Nardus and Sipora would stay on the bus till its arrival at the Joodse Invalide. Nowhere would be safe now, but right now in their situation, this felt like it was the right move.

GOOD-BYE

Marcel Rodrigues needed to do one more thing before he was to take his son and attempt his escape to Switzerland. He needed to see his daughter for what might be one last time.

As he headed for the *Joodse Invalide,* he knew that there was no way of knowing what the future held for any of them. Every move made and every strategy taken by any Jew was a dangerous one at this point. What was safer? Sipora staying behind in the *Joodse Invalide* or he and Bram attempting to flee the country? He did not know, and anyone who thought they did was mistaken, if not delusional.

He and Bram had remained together till now, and unless Bram insisted otherwise, they would continue to remain together. Two men traveling seemed to be the best chance that they had, and with Sipora already in one of those situations that had as much chance of working as any other, having her come along made little to no sense for any of them. The one thing that was certain was that Marcel and Bram could not remain in their home any longer.

Marcel walked up to the entrance of the *Joodse Invalide.* What was once an institution bristling with activity was now quiet and deserted. It was very early morning as he walked in the door. Sipora had let him know what room she was in, so he had no need to speak to anyone else. The few people he passed as he walked down the hall toward the staircase that would take him to his daughter on the second floor showed no alarm or suspicion at his presence. They knew just by looking at him that he was Jewish and therefore no threat to their delicate security.

Marcel walked down the hallway toward Sipora's room. When he reached the door, he knocked on it with enough force for her to hear, but soft enough that she would not be startled.

He heard her voice. "Yes," she said raising her voice slightly. "Come in."

Sipora lay still as her father walked in the room. She had not seen him look this tired and sad since right after her mother had died. He walked up to the bed and put his hand on her head as he spoke to her.

"How are you doing?" he asked.

Sipora smiled as she answered, "I am doing okay. So far we've been safe here. My friend Nardus is doing his best to keep an eye on things; if I have to leave in a hurry, I may have some warning."

"Well, I've come to tell you that Bram and I are leaving Amsterdam and heading for Switzerland," continued Marcel, forcing himself to get to the point. "It's no longer safe for us at home. If anything, we've been lucky we haven't been picked up yet."

Almost pleading as she spoke, Sipora replied, "Nardus said he could get you false papers and help you find a place to hide. You don't have to try to leave the country. It's so dangerous."

Marcel walked toward the window, and as he stared into the distance, he shook his head in disagreement. "No. If we stay here out on the street, it will be too dangerous. We can't stay here. We have to go."

Sipora started to cry. Knowing that the longer this went on, the harder it would be for both of them, Marcel walked backed to the bed, bent over, and kissed Sipora on the forehead.

"I will tell Bram that you are doing well and send him your love. Be safe and healthy. I have to go. We leave tomorrow."

Sipora was worried about her father and brother. There was really nothing she could do. She spoke with Nardus about this. Nardus tried to convince Marcel to allow him to find a hiding place for him and his son. His efforts, however, were fruitless. Marcel felt that his plan to escape to Switzerland would end up better for he and Bram, and that was what he intended to do. Time was running out for Marcel and Bram Rodrigues.

Her place in the hospital at least provided Sipora with some degree of safety. As long as she had some task to fulfill, the chances of her being taken away by the Nazis was smaller than it was for a man and his son, who served no purpose in their eyes. Even though it was apparent that the ultimate goal of the Nazis was to clear all the Jews out of Amsterdam, at least as long as there were hospitals with Jewish patients, a nurse had importance.

But Marcel and Bram served no purpose to the Germans, and with their very Jewish faces, Marcel knew that he had to do something and do it quick.

Even though Marcel trusted Nardus, he felt that the best course of action would be to flee the city and head south, the ultimate goal being Switzerland. Marcel was an accomplished man with much experience, and since he had traveled a lot, he knew his way around. He had been to Switzerland and knew how to get there and what to expect. They would head south, travel through Belgium, and end up in Switzerland. Marcel's logic was sound.

However, these were times when logic held very little meaning.

The next morning Marcel was up at the crack of dawn. There was a train leaving to Maastricht in an hour and a half, and he planned to be on that train with Bram.

Bram was still a young boy, and although he was sweet and kind and well behaved, he was also confused.

"Why do we have to leave, Papi?" he asked Marcel. "I am sure if we stay inside and out of the way, we will be fine."

"Unfortunately, it is not that simple, Bram," replied Marcel. "If we stay they will come into our home and take us away. If we have to leave anyway, let us go somewhere I know we will be comfortable and happy."

They left with one bag each. They could not take much. Marcel knew this. So what he decided was to take just the one bag for each of them. This way maybe they would attract less attention, give less of an appearance of escaping and more of an appearance of a father and son taking a trip.

Before they left the house, Marcel spoke with the housekeeper, Emmy. He informed her of their plans, saying the house was in her charge until things were better and they were able to return.

Central station Amsterdam was busy that morning. This was an advantage for Marcel and Bram. With the crowds of people, they would have a better chance of getting on the train and making it to Maastricht. Once they got to the border town, they would have to travel through Belgium until they reached the safety of the neutral and until now unthreatened Switzerland.

They made it onto the train, and as it pulled away, Marcel knew one thing for sure. If he was to ever get back to Amsterdam, it would not be for a very long time. However, his one concern now was to get himself and his son to safety. He wanted to distance himself from the horrors taking place in his hometown. He was concerned for his daughter Sipora but somehow felt that she was now in no less danger than he and Bram were, and he felt that with Nardus looking after her, she was as safe as one could hope for.

The train ride was relatively peaceful, and there were no Nazi officers on board. Marcel encouraged his young son to close his eyes and get some rest. When he saw that his boy was sleeping, Marcel closed his eyes as well. He rested and prayed, prayed that when the train stopped, they would be able to travel to safety.

Marcel woke with the sound of the train coming to a stop. The train was approaching the station in Maastricht, and Marcel knew this moment would determine their fate. As they got off the train, they began to walk toward the border crossing with the rest of the passengers.

Marcel knew what was about to happen. Every single person at the border was being checked by an SS officer, and it was clear what was happening. Those who looked Jewish were being held to the side and not allowed to cross. Those who had lighter complexions were being allowed to pass.

They reached the front of the line.

"Papieren!" barked the SS officer to Marcel. He looked at the papers, looked at both Marcel and Bram with disdain, and ordered them to stand to the side.

Every person who was told to stand to the side was subsequently transported to a concentration camp, a death camp.

"You two," barked the SS officer at Marcel and Bram, "stop here and stand to the side."

After being stopped at the border, Marcel and Bram were taken to

Belgium, where they were processed by the local Nazi government and transported to their death.

Marcel Rodrigues: Murdered, September 23, 1943, Auschwitz
Abraham Rodrigues: Murdered, September 23, 1943, Auschwitz

THE JOURNEY BEGINS

Till this point, even with all the horror taking place, Sipora had been able to remain in her hometown of Amsterdam. Having lost her father, brother, fiancé, and countless other friends and family, this was of little solace to her, but at least she had not had to travel to find shelter. This too was now going to change. Most Jews still living in Amsterdam were now hiding in safe havens provided by Dutch families willing to risk harm in the name of protecting human life. Many Dutch families exhibited such bravery all over the country, but to do so in Amsterdam would be the greatest of risks. Sipora was about to begin her journey out of Amsterdam, not knowing if and when she would ever return. She would leave the Joodse Invalide and spend 2 weeks in hiding in the home of the grandmother of her good friend Lily before making one final move in Amsterdam. The last place she would be before leaving would be the home of her father's best friend, Jan Van de Berg; when she would leave, she would not be alone.

SAVING REINA

It had been about two weeks since Sipora had left the JoodseInvalide, and the few stragglers that had remained behind knew that within a short time they too would need to be on the move to another location. It had been a few weeks since the last of the packed transports left Amsterdam, and now, with less for them to do, the Nazis were more dangerous to those trying to hide away in the more public locations.

Nardus knew that the next patrol to inspect the *Joodse Invalide* would likely be the most meticulous one yet, and anyone found would be in grave danger. He needed to find a way to get out undetected. Most of the patrols were a collaborative effort between the Green Police and the special battalion the Nazis had set up in the Dutch police force. There was no way Nardus would even consider trying to pass himself off as a Nazi soldier, even if he were able to get hold of one of their uniforms. However, a Dutch police officer was a far more realistic goal.

Of immediate concern to Nardus was the safety of his childhood friend, Reina Van Creveld. Being that she was the director of the hospital, Nardus knew of two relative certainties. First, she would be taken away and treated in a harsher manner than a regular staff member or patient. And second, and this was something Nardus was counting on, she would be the last person the Nazis would come for. Her office was one floor down from Sipora's room, and he knew that there was nowhere else to find her but there. If she had gone from her office, there would be nothing Nardus could do for her.

Nardus hoped that the patrol had not made it up to the second floor yet. His big concern was getting back to Sipora, so as he got to the second floor, he looked around very carefully before proceeding to Reina's office. The door was closed as he got there. He opened up the door and found Reina sitting at her desk, crying and shaking. He understood why, and he felt compassion, but he was not there to comfort her, he was there to save her.

Nardus put his finger to his lips, indicating to her not to speak. He looked around the office, trying to figure out their next move. He walked right up to her and quietly whispered, "That panel there on the ceiling, what does it lead to?"

Reina's eyes moved to the area Nardus was referring to; she stared at it and thought for a few seconds.

"That is the storage closet. It is where we keep bed pans and syringes," she replied with a confused tone. "There is no way out from that area, and besides myself and a few nurses, no one has the key from the outside."

"Perfect," said Nardus, confusing Reina even more. "The way they are, there is no way they will want to be anywhere near a room like that."

He took a chair and, standing near to the ceiling, pushed the panel through. Reina watched as Nardus did a very quick examination of the room right above the panel; she now knew what he planned on doing. He motioned to her to come over to where he was as he got down from the chair.

"Here is what you need to do," he told her. "You will hide in that room. I am as certain as I can be that they will not search there. I will open the window, and when they come in and look around, they will assume that you escaped by jumping out the window."

Reina nodded her head in complete agreement and cooperation with Nardus's plan.

He then looked at her very sternly and said, "Now listen to me carefully, because this is the most important part. You do not come out and you do not respond to anyone. Anyone. The only person you respond to is me. I will come back and get you and take you to people who can help you find a safe place to stay."

Reina was no longer shaking, because her fear had somewhat subsided.

With tears still falling down her face, she looked at Nardus and said, "Thank you so much, my friend."

Never the sentimentalist, Nardus replied, "No need to thank me. Just remember: You respond to no one but me."

Reina climbed through the ceiling into the storage room. Nardus replaced the panel, making sure it looked untouched, opened the windows wide, and left the room, closing the door behind him quietly

To this point, things had gone as Nardus had hoped. With Reina hiding in the storage room, she now had some chance of survival. Her conditions were frightening and uncomfortable, but this was the only way she would not be detected by the soldiers.

Nardus had told Reina he would come back for her as soon as an opportunity presented itself, but right now it wasn't safe for him to stay there. Even with the Dutch policeman's uniform he had commandeered, staying in this building at this moment would do nothing other than arouse suspicion. Nardus needed to get out, come back after dark, and take Reina to a safe location. He then needed to squeeze out one more night's sleep in the *Joodse Invalide* before he left this once remarkable institution behind. His plan was to meet Sipora early in the morning at Jan Van de Berg's home and, in all likelihood, leave Amsterdam.

As arranged, Nardus would later return for Reina and tap on the panel 3 times as a code for her to come out of the storage room. On this day Reina Van Creveld would be safe and she would end up surviving the war.

LEAVING

The Green Police were very active in the area. They had officially completed the deportation of Amsterdam's Jews and, in the process, had left what were once thriving and energetic neighborhoods in ruins. What was once a city rich with Jewish culture was now a horrifying symbol of the proficiency of the Nazi killing machine. All that was left for the Green Police to do was to filter through hospitals, schools, and Jewish neighborhoods and find those that had somehow managed to escape past the Nazi dragnet. Anyone being found at this point in any of these institutions would be in danger of deportation. Nardus could not risk this.

He had his false papers allowing him to get away, but if he stayed here in the *Joodse Invalide*, he was certain it would arouse suspicion. And any degree of suspicion usually resulted in the individual being sent somewhere against their will. Nardus could not let this happen.

After what had been another day filled with horror and tragedy, Nardus was grateful to be at Jan Van de Berg's house, sitting at the dining room table with Sipora and her father's best friend. Although Sipora and Jan had not witnessed firsthand the events which had taken place the way that Nardus had, information had a tendency to reach those who wanted it. They knew of the Green Police combing through neighborhoods and knew that yesterday was another day in which they did their utmost to see to it that no public institution remained a safe haven for any of the Jewish population.

With the intensity and frequency of the raids remaining high, and the time needed to search an area diminishing, it had become more dangerous than ever to remain in Amsterdam.

It was Nardus who was the first to state that which had become obvious to the three of them.

"It is no longer safe for you to be here in Amsterdam," he said, looking at Sipora. "If we stay here, the chances of them finding you are far greater than if we leave the city."

Although he would do anything for his lost friend's little girl, Jan Van de Berg knew Nardus's words were true.

"If I felt otherwise, I would insist you stay here for as long as you want to," he said, looking at Sipora. "I want you to see this as your home. But the random searches of homes are taking place all over the city. You need to find a place where the Nazis aren't congregating and there are fewer searches. That way you can at least have a strategy of how to hide. Here there is none. It's just every day hoping for the best."

Sipora did not have much she wished to say, but seeing the pained look in this man's face, she wanted to make clear to him that she too felt it was the correct move.

"I know I am welcome here, Uncle Jan," she said, referring to him in the close, familiar way she had her entire life. "But I understand the situation. This is where they will be looking, and if they find me, it's over. It will be good to know for certain that there will be someone here if I can make it back."

"I know of a place in Kampen where some Jews are being set up with homes to hide in," said Nardus. "I don't know for sure what to make of it, but at least it's a start. We should leave right away."

Knowing that she now needed to follow Nardus's instructions implicitly, Sipora stood up and said, "Okay. Just give me a few minutes to freshen up and get some things together and I will be ready."

As she walked out of the room, the look on Jan Van de Berg's face changed from comforting to concerned.

"You know that even with that uniform you are wearing, this is going to be a very dangerous trip," he told Nardus.

"I do," replied Nardus in a tone that combined agreement with determination. "But as you said, there is no other choice. If we go, there is a chance she won't make it, but if we stay, there is only a small chance that she will. It's a difficult move to make but an easy decision."

Wishing to express his gratitude and admiration for the young man standing before him, Jan Van de Berg placed his hand on Nardus's shoulder.

"Max would have liked you," he said, referring to Sipora's father by the name those closest often referred to him as. "She's lucky to have found you."

Nardus chuckled slightly and said, "Let's hope so. I'll do my best keep her safe."

Sipora came back into the dining area, carrying a small suitcase. Nardus looked at it and said to her, "You will be carrying your own bag. We will be traveling with you as my prisoner, not as my friend."

"I understand," replied Sipora.

She turned to Jan Van de Berg and once again, as had happened so often in these past months, felt the tears coming into her eyes. "Be careful," she said to him. "And thank you so much for looking after me."

"Just be safe and get back here as soon as it is possible," said Jan. "This situation won't last forever, and when it's over, I'll be here for you. For both of you," he said, as he took Nardus's hand and shook it.

Sipora walked over to Jan Van de Berg and gave him a hug good-bye, hoping it would not be for the last time.

THE TRAIN

Their walk to the train station was brisk and deliberate. Nardus had instructed Sipora that everything that was to happen over the next few hours would depend on appearances. She was to be his prisoner, not his friend or his acquaintance. It needed to be clear to anyone who saw them that he was transporting her in an official capacity and that she was traveling against her will. Anything else would arouse a suspicion that would more than likely not end well for either one of them.

The station was very busy. The train to Kampen was already boarding, and Nardus watched the platform as the passengers, many of them Nazi soldiers, began to get on. He was not having second thoughts, but he knew that sometime within the next few hours they would be confronted with a situation that held grave dangers. He also knew that he would allow neither Sipora nor himself to be taken alive. His instincts, combined with information that had filtered through, made him certain that if they were arrested they would end up dead anyway, so he had no intention of allowing these Nazi barbarians to cause either one of them prolonged suffering. Sipora in particular would have to endure tortures he would not allow. He had the gun he had taken from the former owner of the uniform he was wearing to see to it that if anything went down, it went down on his terms. He would have his hand ready to grab it from the holster on his belt within a second's notice.

Perhaps one of the advantages Nardus had had till now was that whenever confronted with the enemy, he was more prepared than they were. Most if not all of the Nazis soldiers on this train were traveling with no expectation of an incident. Upon boarding the train, Nardus had a look of confident arrogance. He was, after all, meant to be a Dutch policeman transporting a Jewish woman to a camp for processing. Sipora's appearance was more in line with how she felt: frightened and anxious. Nardus told Sipora she did not have to control her fear. He did not want her to feel it, but being that he was meant to be taking her away for purposes detrimental to her well-being, a look of fear on her face would not be suspicious. If anything, it would make the scenario more believable.

Nardus had briefed Sipora on some important issues. Under no circumstances was she ever to appear amused or comfortable. And he warned her that there was a very good chance he would say some demeaning things about her, right in front of her face. They were to have no conversation other than her responding when addressed by either himself, a Nazi soldier, or a member of the Green Police.

They boarded the train and entered a car with somewhere between fifteen and twenty soldiers, including some higher ranked officers. Nardus knew that the other cars had a good chance of having a similar amount, if not more, and that leaving this car would be contrary to the image he was trying to create. He was supposed to be a Dutch collaborator traveling with a Jewish woman to a destination that would not fare well for her.

Nardus found two seats not that far from where a group of Nazis were sitting and instructed Sipora to sit down. Nardus sat down and took a cigarette out of the inside pocket of his leather jacket. He was glad the Dutch policeman he had accosted for his uniform was a smoker. It was a bonus he had not expected. He sat there, alert yet forcing himself to relax. The calmer he looked, the less it would appear as though he had something to hide.

Nardus was not scared. Somehow he never was, but when danger was near, his mind focused in a way that most others would not be able to. He was alert to every image and sound around him and had a sense of what was going to happen. So when three German soldiers stood up, he knew that they were coming his way, and he was ready. He extinguished his cigarette to free up both hands but continued to look out the window, as he had been doing for the past few minutes. As they approached their seats, never glancing at Sipora, he turned to the three soldiers, one of which was an officer, now standing in fronting of him. The officer spoke.

"What's going on here?" he asked, with an intimidating, but nonthreatening tone. "What are you doing with this … Jew?" He looked at Sipora with disdain, pausing before saying "Jew" to further stress his disgust.

"She is my prisoner," replied Nardus. "I am taking her to the north and will bring her to the camp with the rest of the Jews."

"Let me see your papers," continued the officer.

Nardus stood up, followed the officer's orders, and presented his papers, this time the ones with the name of Jan Henraat, and then he produced papers for Sipora as well. The officer glanced over the papers and handed them back to Nardus, his expression never changing.

"Where are you taking her exactly?" asked the officer.

This was the moment Nardus had been expecting and had attempted to prepare Sipora for as best he could.

"I will eventually take her to the north," he said. "To Westerbork or Amersfoort. Or I will just drop her off if I find a transport going that way. I was just stopping to see some friends first and thought I would have some fun before I got rid of her."

The officer seemed somewhat amused by this, and shaking his head, he turned to the other soldiers.

"He wants to have some fun," he said, chuckling slightly as he did.

Taking the lead from the officer, one of the soldiers cocked his pistol.

"Maybe we should have the fun instead, *ya*?" he said with the arrogance and confidence he had gained after the officer had addressed him.

Nardus knew that this was no moment to show weakness. He needed to gamble and confront them. It was not a bluff. He would fight them if necessary, but with more than ten other soldiers sitting behind them, he knew that he would not win. He was just going to make certain that if there was a conflict, he would lose on his terms. He pushed his jacket open, exposed his pistol, and removed it from his holster.

"She's my prisoner, and if you want her, you are going to have to take her from me," he said, holding his pistol low but clearly in the direction of the officer. Now the soldier knew that should he react, he would be responsible for the shooting of his superior and would find himself in a serious mess. He would therefore be more cautious about shooting Nardus.

For about fifteen seconds, they all stood there. Some of the other soldiers, seeing a situation brewing, rose from their seats. Both Nardus and the soldier kept their guns in the same position. Nardus knew, as he would always know, that in moments of negotiation, no matter what the consequences, the first person to speak would almost always be the one to lose. So he waited.

"Put down your gun," the officer said as he turned to the soldier next to him. And then turning back to Nardus, he said, "You've got balls, man. We need more Dutchmen like you on our side." He looked briefly at Sipora with irreverence and amusement, and then he turned back to Nardus and said, "Even a Jew can be good for something, *ya?*"

Disgusted at the men standing in front of him but relieved with the outcome, Nardus forced a chuckle. "*Ya,*" he said. "Is there anything else?"

"No," replied the officer. "I trust you will see to it that she ends up like the rest of them. Carry on."

As the three walked away, Nardus stole a quick glance at Sipora, her pale face revealing the fear she was feeling. Nardus once again reached for a cigarette, lit it, and stared out the window.

THE NIGHT IN THE BARN

When the train arrived in Kampen, Nardus knew he was supposed to get to the house of someone by the name of Schapman, where they would be able to spend the night and be transported to a safe location in the morning. A somewhat shady character, Schapman dabbled in black market activities and was the type of individual always looking for an angle. Bottom line for him was whether or not he could make a profit. He was supposed to have shown up at Jan Van de Berg's house, but never made it, something that alerted Nardus to a possible situation developing.

Nardus and Sipora arrived to find the upper floor of Schapman's home filled with twenty to thirty other Jewish people who were doing nothing but sitting around and waiting. Nardus wondered what they were waiting for. Something about this situation was very wrong. First of all, his instinct was always to avoid groups, and this group was more problematic than any he had seen. Something was amiss here. He knew this for sure. He turned to Sipora and said, with no hesitation or room for debate, "We're leaving."

After leaving Schapman's house in a hurry, Nardus and Sipora were less concerned with where they were going and more concerned with staying on the move. If Nardus was correct about his suspicions, the first matter at hand was getting away from there as quickly as possible. This meant that they needed to leave the area immediately and just keep going.

Walking didn't scare either one of them. Growing up in Holland, they would regularly walk thirty minutes to an hour each way just to get to school. Being on the move and walking a long way was not something they anticipated would cause problems for either one of them.

But it wasn't the potential distance that made this walk different. This wasn't like a walk to school or a walk to see friends on a Saturday or Sunday. There was nothing routine about this trip. This wasn't a walk they had planned or chosen, and it was not a walk they could postpone for another day.

Nardus was fairly certain that this was a walk away from danger, and therefore they needed to walk quickly, at least in the beginning.

Once they created some distance between themselves and Schapman's house, they could ease up a little. But until then, there was no stopping and no getting caught. Sipora looked like a Jew, and to anyone who saw her, she would stand out as someone who needed to get away in order to avoid detection from German soldiers or any of the Dutch who sympathized with the Nazi movement and occupation.

Although it was not clear whether this man traveling with her was transporting her or protecting her, it still was a less than ordinary sight and, therefore, would attract attention. In the event that they were caught, aiding and abetting a Jew, in the eyes of the German occupiers, made him at least as guilty as if he actually were a Jew.

Ironically, Nardus, someone who grew up much more active in Judaism than Sipora, could have avoided these dangers he found himself in today. All he had to do was to remain on his own, live as Jan Henraat, and avoid this woman who so obviously would not have the same ability to avoid capture that he would. He could have easily steered away from any impending danger rather than stay with her.

Not only was Nardus not going to do this, he never even considered it. The danger didn't scare him, and the truth was that he just didn't care. He knew what he wanted, and he knew how he felt. He was not afraid of the situation and was focused only on the matter at hand: getting Sipora to safety.

By now, Nardus's instincts had become so sharp that the slightest doubt caused him to avoid a situation, and Sipora, who now had committed to putting her life in Nardus's hands, was not going to question his decisions.

As time went on, trusting Nardus and listening to him became easier. He had done nothing other than help her and saved her life to this point.

What made this even easier was that Sipora's feelings had started to change. The way Nardus had looked after her, from the time they had met until now, trust was not in question anymore. Her intentions had not been the same as his throughout the ordeal, but he had, nevertheless, done nothing but treat her with respect and kindness. Now she was starting to feel something different. She was lonely and sad, and here was a man who, at this moment, had become the only thing in her life she could be certain of. Even in Sipora's optimistic and idealistic eyes, the future was at worst bleak, and at best filled with question marks. She had come close to giving up so many times, but this man would not let her do so. This man, Nardus, was imposing his will on Sipora. And Sipora knew that allowing him to was the only choice she had. In giving herself over to him in the name of her safety, she was now starting to feel a different sort of closeness to him, one that gave her a little more comfort.

Nardus was by no means a soft man. Never prone to sentimentalism, he was not one to make decisions based on romantic considerations. He would see a situation, spend some time analyzing it, and leave the rest to his gut. If he felt something was off, he would respect that feeling, something that till now had served him well and helped them survive.

Nardus felt he was alive today for two reasons, the first and foremost being good fortune. Although he had no choice but to live a life without Jewish practice while avoiding German detection, he was still a man of strong belief, and it was his belief that the reason God had allowed him to live was not because he was better, but because he was lucky. He thought of those who had been taken. His mother and father; his sister Elizabeth and her husband Aaron; Sipora's father and little brother Bram; these were all people he would think of and realize that he was not better, just more fortunate to this point to have survived. He was a realist and knew that the chances of ever seeing any of these people again were slim at best.

The second reason Nardus had made it this far was that he trusted no one. He knew that not everyone who would turn on another did so in the name of an evil agenda or personal gain. Some would do so out of fear. The second group was a far more dangerous group, because fear could cause good people to do bad things. And when dealing with bad people, things were a lot less uncertain than when dealing with good people doing bad. Nardus knew that when a Nazi soldier banged on a door, you wouldn't need much insight to suspect imminent treachery and danger. However, an invitation from someone who was inherently decent, but scared for his life, presented a far greater danger, one in which the only truly useful weapon was suspicion. Nardus had known this instinctively on some level already, but now he had chosen to turn it into a tool and prerequisite. It didn't make Nardus the most enjoyable man to be around, but this wasn't about enjoyment, this was about survival. It was this basic principle that helped Nardus decide that they should leave Schapman's for safer shelter. It was for this reason both he and Sipora were now once again on the move.

As was so often the case, the Dutch air was damp and cold. Nardus could tell this was getting more and more difficult on Sipora. They had been walking for a couple of hours now. They had been in a relatively warm spot and had left it in order to move on. Sipora was tired. She wanted a place to stop and rest her weary body. She had wanted to protest Nardus's decision to leave Schapman's house but knew by now that he knew what he was doing and was right more often than he was wrong. Besides, he wouldn't have listened to her anyway.

Sipora needed to stop for a bit. Seeing this, Nardus took her hand and walked over toward a gigantic oak tree off the side of the road.

"Let's rest against this tree for a few minutes," he said.

This was music to Sipora's ears. There had been so many moments that had felt like eternities in the past few years that she had forgotten some already, but she did not feel she would forget this one.

"Do you think we will find a place to sleep tonight?" she asked Nardus.

"I certainly hope so," he replied, "but we can't be reckless just because we're tired."

Although he was not tired, Nardus said this in order to make it seem as though he understood how she felt. In reality, he had no concerns about when they would rest and was too alert to be tired. In one day, they had traveled on a train filled with German soldiers and had come and gone from what felt like an insecure house of a black market merchant. Sure, he would be happy to stop and rest and maybe even get something to eat, but too much had happened that day to be foolish in the name of exhaustion. So he had decided that they were just going to walk as long as it took to find a place that seemed safe or felt right.

"I'm not complaining," said Sipora. "I know that being safe is the most important thing and that you know what you're doing."

This was the first time she had expressed to Nardus her unconditional trust. He knew she trusted him. That was obvious. They had come so far together already, and he had certainly proven himself to her. But until now there was always this impression that she was following him somewhat reluctantly, as if she was with him because she had no better alternative than to stay with him. A woman alone, needing a friend. Now it felt a little different. Now in some ways, she wanted to be with him. Now they were two people together.

Sensing this, Nardus gave her the only thing he had to offer at this moment: hope.

"I promise you we will find a place to rest soon and that we will keep moving until we find somewhere that you will be safe," he said. "There will be people here willing to take us in for a night. It's just a matter of time."

They began walking again. Sipora now had her arm through Nardus's. She sensed some surprise on his part when she took hold of it, but certainly sensed no objection. She certainly did like having him to hold on to as she got more and more tired from the walk, but this was about more than that. She was feeling safe around him, and the closer she got, the safer she felt. The possible ramifications in feeling this were not lost on her, but she wasn't going to make that an issue. She was just relieved that she felt some comfort in these very unpleasant times.

As they continued to walk, Nardus saw what appeared to be a farm in the distance. It was dark, though, and it was possible that his eyes were playing tricks on him. As they got closer, it became clear that what he had thought was a structure was actually just a cluster of trees. He was feeling some frustration now. They had been walking for a while, and he wanted to stop. He didn't like being out in the open, exposed like this. He felt safer and more in control walking in the daylight, where he could see a distance before them.

After passing the trees, they turned a small corner. Now there was no mistaking what he saw. They both saw it. In front of them, maybe a thousand feet ahead, was a light in the window of a house.

"You see that light?" Nardus asked Sipora.

She nodded slowly. She knew that there was no guarantee that this would be where they would stop. "I do," she replied softly. "What do you think we should do?"

Nardus wanted to stop but knew they needed to be careful. "We will go up toward the house carefully and make sure nothing looks suspicious. The Nazis have taken over a lot of homes. There is no guarantee this is not one of them. However, I am more concerned with how these people will react to seeing your Jewish face."

They continued at the same pace. They did not let the excitement of seeing the home in the distance take control of them. They knew that if something looked wrong, they would need to keep moving, and maybe even get away at a quicker pace. So they continued at the steady pace they had been on for some time now.

They got up to the door of the house, and when they saw the name on the door, they stopped suddenly. Nardus saw it first and looked toward Sipora and smiled, saying to her, "You see this? It's a good sign. It guarantees nothing but right now I am very happy to take any sign we can get. And this is a good one. I think we may have found our place for the night."

Sipora nodded and smiled in agreement, saying nothing. She too saw this as a good sign. The name on the door was the same as her father's friend; the name brought some immediate comfort and at least the illusion of safety. The name on the door was Van de Berg.

THE INTIMACY BEGINS

Although Sipora lay on her back with her eyes shut, she was still very much awake. So many thoughts were racing through her head. It was not so long ago that she was engaged to marry Hans. They were going to plan their wedding and live a good life together. She had a degree of physical intimacy with Hans, being that they were in love and planning to get married. However, neither of them had any intention of consummating the relationship before their betrothals. This was how it was done in good families in the 1930s and 1940s, and Sipora never had any problem with this. It was never an issue. They would be married, and only then would they fully live as man and wife.

That was then, and this was now. The man lying next to her was not Hans and was not her husband. The man lying next to her was Nardus. The man who had brought her through hell and stayed with her.

After Joop Van de Berg had let them into the house, he was kind enough to provide them with a little bit of food and offered them both shelter. Sipora was to stay in a spare room in the house, and Nardus was to stay in the barn. In the morning, Van de Berg was going to take Sipora to an acquaintance that was looking for help on his ship. He knew the man was looking for a woman to keep the ship clean and organized; Van de Berg was confident that the man would not care that Sipora was Jewish. They were to go there first thing in the morning, but first they would get a decent night's sleep.

There had been a feeling between Nardus and Sipora that was new to them both. They did not want to be apart, but they were not given the option. Van de Berg had decided they should be separated. What he did not know was that Nardus and Sipora had arranged that she would leave the window open so that he could come into her room. So forty-five minutes or so after everyone had said good night, and after the lights had dimmed in the Van de Berg household, Nardus quietly snuck from the barn and walked around the house till he found the open window he was looking for.

He knew this window meant a lot more than just a way into the house. This open window could very well change things forever. Till now, despite his strong feelings for Sipora, Nardus knew that he had just been a guardian for her. In many ways, he was her savior and friend and nothing else. He was fine with that, because this was not something she had asked from him, this was something he had chosen to do. He was in love with her, a kind of love that at this point in time required no reciprocity, just an openness toward him necessary to allow him to do what needed to be done. As commanding and in control as he had been regarding their movements, Nardus was not at all forceful or demanding when it came to any degree of affection from Sipora. Yes, he wanted her, but he was not going to push her. He first wanted to make sure she was safe. Only then would he concern himself with their relationship.

Many things had changed, however. This day that started in one Van de Berg's house and ended in another's, had been filled with so many potential life-changing events that he and Sipora were different people than they had been when they had woken up. Emotions had changed, attitudes were adjusted, and all logic had been altered. Their lives were different, their feelings were different, and their perceptions would likely never be the same. Nardus knew when he found the open window that what would take place would be a lot more than sex. The consummation of this relationship would go beyond sex. It would be a bond that would tie them together for as long as they would live. And tonight, after the events of a very long day, neither one of them knew how long that would be.

Right and wrong had taken on new meaning in their world. Before the Nazi occupation, people lived freely. People were not arrested just for being what they were, and people were not randomly beaten and killed. The Nazi occupation had changed everything. Right and wrong? This was now about life and death. Good and evil. Neither Sipora nor Nardus knew what tomorrow would bring. They knew that the chances of being dead were as good as the chances of being alive. And they knew that tonight they had each other. Nardus felt calm and alive. Sipora felt comforted and safe. Two years ago, sleeping next to a man who was not her husband, in the house of strangers, and having reached the pinnacle of intimacy would have been wrong. Tonight it was right. Especially with the uncertainty of tomorrow.

This was about something a lot more important than sex, far more important than Sipora losing her virginity. This was about life and about hope. If they were to go on, it was going to be together.

But first they both needed to survive.

KEEP MOVING

Morning came, and Sipora opened her weary but somewhat rested eyes. She looked out the window. As powerful as nature can be, it can also be somewhat deceptive. With the sounds of the birds chirping, the dog barking, and the cows mooing in the pasture, everything seemed so normal.

For a brief time, Sipora lay there and let herself believe everything in the world was right again. But she knew better. Later this morning, Van de Berg would take her to the man who needed help on his boat. Nardus had left at the crack of dawn to pick up a bag of personal items she had left at Schapman's; hopefully, he would be back in time to see her off on the next stage of her journey. More uncertainty, possibly more danger, certainly more fear. Life was anything but normal.

Nardus left the barn at first light and began to walk as the darkness in the sky started to fade. He knew that by the time he reached Schapman's, it would be daylight, and he would be able to see his way around better. It also helped knowing where he was going. He now roughly knew how long he would be walking, and even more importantly, where he would be returning to. He missed Sipora's company, but there was a benefit in not having her with him as well. He was able to move more freely with less concern of a confrontation of any kind with German or collaborating Dutch officials. And he could move faster. It felt like he was walking twice as fast as when he and Sipora had made this trek. He missed her company, but this was a distinct advantage, and he intended to take advantage of it.

Walking alone gave Nardus the opportunity to think. He thought about yesterday. What a day it had been. They had experienced so much in one day that he hardly could believe it all even happened. If someone had told him that in one day, he would have taken Sipora out of Amsterdam, confronted Nazi officers on a train, felt the atmosphere of danger that he had felt in Schapman's, and ended up the day in bed and intimate with Sipora at an entirely different location, he would have told that person their imagination had gotten the better of them. Yet nevertheless, that is what had happened, and Nardus was actually very pleased that he had not known of it sooner. It made him realize that not being prophetic was actually a blessing, for if one did know what was going to happen, it would most likely make it even harder to handle. Nardus was a strong man who till now had shown the ability to handle most of what life was handing him. He decided that part of that was the ability to react and deal with it as it came; he did not want to know the future, just deal with the present and learn from the past. As he walked, he was hopeful that maybe one day he would have children he could share this new understanding with.

Children. Would it ever be? He let himself dream a little, thinking of his childhood and the wonderful experiences growing up in Amsterdam. He thought of Shabbat at home and how he would walk with his friends from one synagogue to another. He thought of his brothers and sisters. Would he ever see any of them again? He knew nothing of the whereabouts of his brothers Meyer and David and their wives Roe and Martha. He knew they had been picked up and that Martha was pregnant, but he did not know where they had ended up. Fie was with Jacques, and although no one was safe, there were very few people he'd rather see looking after someone close to him than the man who had already helped him so much and tried so hard to help his parents.

His parents. He thought about the Saturday nights, after Shabbat, when his father would sit back, smile, and light his cigar. This was a man who lived that old Rabbinical adage, "Who is the wealthy man? The man who is happy with his portion." And he thought of his mother, the quiet, strong woman who gave them all so much and supported her husband through life, and now most likely, through death.

No, Nardus did not want to know the future. What was to come most likely would be difficult enough even without the need to think about it in advance. His instinct would serve him well, and after that, he would just have to depend on luck.

Whether it was luck or his instinct that brought him there, when he arrived in Kampen, he came across Schapman's neighbor; Nardus had seen him standing on his porch when he and Sipora had arrived yesterday. Nardus sized him up quickly and knew this was a decent man. He saw some degree of disapproval in the man's face, but the knowing nod they had exchanged gave Nardus the feeling that it was more directed toward Schapman himself and his questionable activities than it was toward the desperate souls entering into his home. As he walked up to him, this feeling was about to be confirmed.

The neighbor called Nardus "jonge," the Dutch word for "boy," which was used to establish trust or a connection. "What are you doing back here, jonge?" he asked. "And where is the woman who was with you?"

"She is safe," replied Nardus. "We found a place to stay last night further out in the countryside. But we left in a hurry last night and she left her bag. I've come back to get it."

"Well, it is good that you did not stay; do not go another step," continued the man. "All the people who were there are dead. Shot. They were ambushed on the boat by a Nazi patrol. The whole thing was a set up. Just get out of here quickly and don't look back."

Nardus was not surprised. He knew something was wrong last night. That is why they left as quickly as they did. Now he had to worry not only about whether anyone had spoken of them being there, but whether the German patrols were still in the vicinity.

Nardus knew one thing for certain: Neither he nor Sipora could stay in the area. It would be too dangerous. As much as he was uncomfortable with the idea of leaving her with another strange man, he knew that she'd be hard to stumble across while on a moving boat. He would have his concerns and questions about the owner of the boat, but if she was there, at least the majority of his concerns would be limited to him. Stationary in a barn, with a reluctant host, would make her much more exposed; it was a less secure option. She would go on the boat. He would get back in time just to let the man know someone was concerned about her whereabouts and that there was no free rein with her, but he would let her go.

The next question for Nardus was where he would go. He could not roam around the countryside, hoping for random jobs and places to stay. The Nazis were rounding up young, healthy man and transporting them to Germany to do the most difficult labor. Nardus wasn't worried about the labor, but he did not want to go to Germany. He needed to stay in Holland and be as near to Sipora as possible.

He had heard of a labor camp in the polders. The Germans had indicated that men who were working on projects in Holland would be able to stay in Holland. This would be perfect for Nardus. He would have resting quarters, at least minimal sustenance, and a guarantee he would stay in Holland. He would see Sipora off and then make his way north to the polders and volunteer his services.

Particularly under the circumstances, Joop Van de Berg had been a very gracious host. He had provided shelter for both Nardus and Sipora, had made sure they were not hungry, and was clearly someone who wanted no harm to come to either one of them. There was no question that they had been fortunate last night. This was a decent man. He had welcomed them for the night and gave them the brief respite they had so desperately needed. But Joop Van de Berg , as decent as he was, wanted no part of this war. Keeping anyone there for any extended period of time had involved him in a way he had no desire to be. So although he wished both Sipora and Nardus well, it was now time for them both to move on.

Jan Boekman was not exactly someone Joop Van de Berg called a friend, but he had known him for a long time. If Boekman needed some supplies or tools from the farm, he would come to Van de Berg. Van de Berg would not need Boekman's help often, but on occasions in which he wanted to travel to a location best reached by boat, Boekman would take him there. Van de Berg had had enough dealings and conversations with Boekman to know this was a man who had no love for the Germans and their occupation. He was a religious man who saw the activities taking place in cities and villages throughout Holland. These Germans were godless barbarians, and he would do nothing to help them in their cause.

Boekman was happy to hear Van de Berg had someone to help him out on the boat. He had no criteria other than someone who would cooperate with him and not cause him any trouble. And he certainly had no problem with the fact that she was clearly Jewish. She was young, attractive, and clearly ready to do the necessary tasks. She would do fine, as long as it was understood that this other man approaching with his friend and the woman was not coming on board as well.

Van de Berg walked toward the boat with Nardus and Sipora. They were now maybe thirty feet away. He stopped and turned toward them. "Please wait for me here while I speak with him and let him know about you," Van de Berg instructed Sipora. "He told me what he was looking for, so I am sure it will be fine, but it is his boat and I just need to explain the situation to him. I'll be very honest with you. He is a very Calvinistic, conservative man and not a huge fan of the Jews. I know this because I have heard him speak about this particular subject many times. However, his feelings are religious and deep seated. He may think the religion is wrong, but he feels that killing the people is worse. So although he won't exactly encourage your Jewish way of life, and I advise you not to debate him on its merits, trust me, this man has no love for the Germans and their methods. She may spend weeks hearing about how the Jews killed his Lord, but he won't turn her over to the Germans. She'll be safe."

As Van de Berg walked away, Nardus sized up Boekman the same way he did with every stranger he came across. This was one of those times when he was not too thrilled with what he saw. Boekman was not the cleanest of men, he was awkward in his movements, and he had the look on his face of an angry man. Nardus did not like this man, but he knew there wasn't any other safe option right now. The other thing was that Nardus had learned to be a lot more wary of people who seemed fine than ones who had clearly unpleasant characteristics. It was basic logic. If this man had the worst of intentions, he would likely put on some type of front in an attempt to seem harmless. Boekman put up no front. The time ahead of Sipora was not going to be pleasant. Be that as it may, comfort and pleasure could not be priorities right now. The only thing that mattered right now was safety.

He looked toward Sipora. He could see and feel her discomfort. She felt like a package being dropped off. She knew this was for the best, and she knew Nardus would not let her stay unless it was the right move, but nevertheless it was an unpleasant situation to the say the least. All it did was to bring her back to the reality she had escaped slightly only a few hours ago. It reminded her of the cold, hard facts. They were at war, and she was a target.

SPEGT

As would be the case so often during these times, Nardus and Sipora had no idea when and if they would see each other again. Nardus knew he needed to say something to Sipora. He had the words ready when Sipora opened her mouth to speak instead.

"Where will you go?" she asked Nardus. "You need to be careful. You can't just continue to roam around from house to house."

"That is not my plan," he replied. "I am going to go to the polders and work. I'll have a place to sleep, some food to eat, and I won't have to worry about being shipped to Germany. I will come back here as often as I can to see you."

"You be careful too," he said quietly but sternly. "It looks like you won't be in any immediate danger here, but you always need to keep your eyes open for anything out of the ordinary. And I want you to promise me one thing."

"What's that?" Sipora asked. Her tone was somewhat confused and anxious.

Nardus looked at her and, with his typical commanding tone, replied, "Tell me everything that happens. If you see something suspicious or out of the ordinary, I want to know about it."

Sipora agreed to Nardus's request. A smile came across her face. Even while being apart from her, he was going to try to keep her safe. There might not have been anything he could actually do while being hours away from her, but his determination and insistence gave her added confidence nonetheless.

Van de Berg walked up to them.

"It's all set," he said with a somewhat relieved tone to his voice. Nodding toward Sipora, he continued, "He made a point of saying that there is only room for her. He said he did not want his wife and children exposed to the wrong behaviors. Like I said, conservative, not the most pleasant, but you'll be safe. She can go on right now. No need to wait."

Nardus and Sipora looked at each other. He took hold of Sipora's hand and was the first to speak this time.

"I know where to find you," he said. "I do not know how often I will get here, but be certain, I will be back."

"Okay Jan," Sipora said calmly, using Nardus's alias. "Be safe and do not worry about me. I will be safe, and I have no doubt from the look of this ship I will have plenty to keep me occupied."

They let go of each other's hands, and Sipora turned and walked toward the boat. More uncertainty lay ahead, but again, all that mattered was that they were still alive and, at least for now, seemingly out of harm's way. Nardus waved good-bye to Sipora, bid Van de Berg well, and then he too was on his way.

Next stop for him: the polders.

Man against the sea. Life was so much simpler when looking at it from that perspective. Holland was filled with low lying bodies of water that were perilous to so many towns and villages as well as the residents living in them. Nardus spent his days working to secure one of these areas. He was working with a crew solidifying the Nordoost (Northeast) Polder on and around the territory known as Schokland, an island in the province of Flevoland. It was purely manual labor, be it moving concrete or shoveling sand, and there was no mental pressure in the work he was doing.

Work had begun on the Nordoost Polder earlier in the year and was just now getting close to the achievement of the ultimate goal. The idea was to reclaim the land from the water and secure it with a series of dikes. Most of the land being worked on by the crew Nardus had joined was surrounding Schokland. The land would, in essence, replace the water, and subsequently Schokland would no longer be an island. Being where it was geographically, it would wind up being part of the municipality of Kampen.

Nardus only needed to be concerned with the performance of the tasks set out for him by his supervisors. The work was basically mindless and free of responsibility. This of course did not mean he was relaxed by any means. He wanted to get back to see Sipora as soon as possible, and he spent much of the time assessing the opportunities to get away. They were rather numerous. They were not prisoners there, and even though they were supervised by German soldiers, they were clearly in an environment with low level security.

He planned on going to see Sipora by the end of the week. He would go and spend a day with her. He saw others coming and going and decided to follow their pattern. In many ways, the work and the accompanying barracks gave this a feel of a small village, except this was a village with no women, children, or men over forty.

Nardus would strike up the occasional conversation, partially to pass the time, but also to see what he could learn about what was going on. The men who were there were an interesting mix from all over the region. Some of the men were clearly manual laborers, the type who were used to this type of work and found it to be the best way to continue the life that they knew. Others were from more intellectual or educated backgrounds and were clearly there for the same reason Nardus was: lack of options.

On breaks, the men would stand around behind the barracks. The barracks were right off the road, and visitors found it rather easy to wander in for various reasons. Peddlers came by with cigarettes or alcohol in exchange for whatever money the men had on them.

Nardus(far left) outside the barracks in Schokland

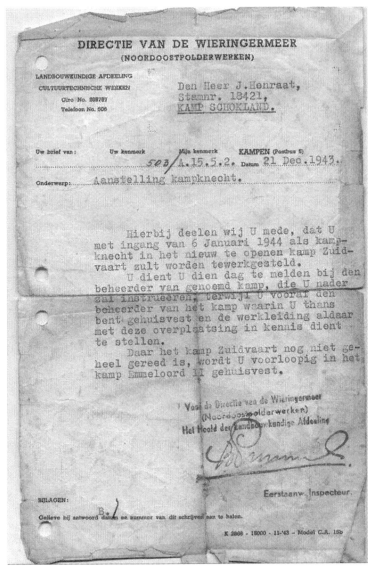

Certificate stating that Nardus was a worker in Schokland

Money had a new meaning for almost everyone at this point. You didn't name your price. If someone had what you wanted, and you had a few pennies, most likely the transaction would go through. This arrangement usually suited both parties and was a somewhat common occurrence here in the Nordoost Polder.

There were various ministers that would come by regularly from the churches in villages near Schokland. One was a Minister Vogelaar, head of a church in a small village near the town of Ommen. Nardus had engaged him in some conversation in order to get some feel for the situation in town and, more importantly, throughout the rest of the country.

Vogelaar was a very decent man who had managed to gain the trust of local officials and even some German officers. He was rich with information and had every intention of using it for as much good as possible without risking his safety or the safety of others around them. This meant that any information needed to be shared discreetly and selectively.

Nardus understood how this worked and, as a result, knew that it would be wise to establish a relationship with the minister. He also had to make sure to somehow let him know who he was and where he stood on the situation in Holland, without giving away too much. It was a delicate balance. Too many details would make him a potential danger, one that at best he would stay away from. Too few details would make him insignificant and not worth risking information on.

One damp, cold day, Nardus was standing near the barracks, smoking a cigarette that one of his coworkers had been generous enough to offer him. On the street not too far away, he saw Minister Vogelaar walking with a tall, thin, blonde man. Nardus had seen this man a few times and wanted to find out more about him. Whoever he was, he seemed confident in walking out in the open and clearly speaking freely. Nardus had a feeling this man was important somehow and decided to take this opportunity to speak with Minister Vogelaar and maybe meet this intriguing stranger. He walked up to them, addressing Vogelaar first.

"Good afternoon, Minister," he said. And then turning to the stranger, Nardus continued, "Sir, I apologize for the interruption, but I wonder if either of you have heard anything about the situation in Amsterdam."

The stranger remained quiet. It was Vogelaar who spoke. Not knowing what Nardus knew, he began with the most basic of information.

"Well, the Germans have occupied the entire city and are sweeping through neighborhoods, conducting raids. Primarily Jewish neighborhoods."

Nardus decided to go out on a limb here. He needed information and knew that he would get nothing without giving something.

"I come from Amsterdam," he offered. "I left in a hurry and wanted to help a friend. I fear it may be too late."

Nardus noticed that his last sentence caused the stranger to turn his head toward him, with piercing eyes. He clearly was sizing Nardus up and, given the situation, had no need to be subtle about it. Knowing the chess game going on, Nardus knew he had only one move. To back up.

"Anyway, gentlemen, if you hear anything important or hear of people needing any assistance, please let me know," he said.

While Minister Vogelaar nodded and thanked Nardus, the stranger next to him stood quietly. Knowing something was more than as it seemed with this man who had approached them, he extended his hand to Nardus, saying, "The name's Spegt. And I am sure we will meet again soon."

JEW FACE

It had been dark for a few hours now as Sipora lay on her cot in the far corner of the boat. Although Boekman's wife and children had gone to bed, he himself was still awake. Sipora could hear him rustling about on the ship's deck.

This first week and a half or so had not been easy at all. There was something very strange about this arrangement. The wife and children hardly interacted with Sipora. It was as though they were warned to keep their distance from this not-so-welcome woman in their midst. Other than an occasional request from his wife, Boekman was the only one who addressed Sipora with any type of regularity. And when he did so, it was generally to bark an order or to make an inappropriate comment.

This was not a nice man, thought Sipora. Yes, he was giving her a safe haven, but he did so at a price. He would regularly belittle Sipora, commenting on her helplessness and weaknesses. When he wasn't doing that, he would bark orders at her or say things to make her feel even more uncomfortable.

Sipora was not one to get into conflict, especially knowing that she needed this place for food and shelter. However, she was prepared to move the cot where she slept as far away from Boekman and his family as space would permit. In this case, it was all the way to the opposite side of the boat. Some of Boekman's comments regarding her looks or her vulnerability made Sipora feel that she needed to send a message back. She could not and would not fight him, but by moving the cot as far away from where he slept as possible, she was making it clear to him that she was there to clean and cook and that he should expect nothing else from her.

Mornings were the easiest time for Sipora because of the speed at which they moved. The mother would be busy attending to the children, and Boekman would find some type of maintenance on the boat to keep him busy. On some days, he had left the boat in the morning and returned with food and supplies for his family. Sipora was not starving, but it was clear that first Boekman fed his family, and whatever scraps were left over were given to Sipora.

Sipora tried hard not to think about what was happening here. Even though she was not living in the fear of the soldiers with guns, her living conditions were anything but ideal. It took every ounce of strength she had to maintain her composure in front of Boekman and his family, but she knew she needed to be strong when they were around. Any significant sign of weakness would only compromise her situation more than it already was.

Sometimes at night, lying alone on the cot, everything would feel like too much for Sipora, and she would begin to sob for what her life had become. Nothing that she had in her past would bring her any solace. If anything, thinking of what she had and what she lost only increased the feeling of despair. Right now, the only person she could think of and find some degree of comfort in was Nardus. At least he could come back. He had gone to do what he had to do to get through this time as well, but he had not been taken. She knew that when he had a chance to get away, he would come her way and see her. She also knew that he would not be able to stay. This too made Sipora sad. Although she was certain that if he could get to her he would, she also knew that whatever time she might have with Nardus would be short-lived. But at least it gave her something to look forward to.

It was now midmorning, and Sipora had her first break of the day. As had been the routine so far, everyone had eaten, and Sipora had cleaned up after everyone's meal and proceeded to tidy up the Boekmans' bedroom and make all the beds. On some days, she would stand on deck and look out at the water, and on other days she would look out at the road and glance over the countryside. Today was a day to gaze at the green pastures and animals in the distance.

Sipora always had a fondness for the natural beauty her country had to offer. The beautiful landscaping, the large strong trees with their elegant leaves blowing in synchronized patterns, combined with the grace of the horses and innocence of the cows, all were part of the charm and grace that was Holland. Taking a moment to stop and see as much of this as possible always gave Sipora some comfort. She put her head down, feeling somewhat relaxed and at ease by these moments of inner escape.

She raised her head and saw a figure moving in the distance. As the figure got closer, she saw it was a man, and as he came still closer, she recognized who this man was. It was Nardus. She smiled for what felt like the first time in almost two weeks. He had come to see her.

One day about two weeks later, it was damp and miserable on Boekman's boat. With the rain falling slightly, the air was cold and unpleasant. Sipora was working on the deck when in the distance she saw a boat heading up the river. As the boat passed them, she saw two Nazi officers on board, one with a pair of binoculars in his hands. She could see the binoculars were pointed at her; turning away at this point would do nothing but invite a search of Boekman's boat, so she just looked back. She was frightened, but at least if she looked, she would know what was going on.

She could not see the face of the German officer as he could see hers, but she saw as his lips moved and he uttered the words that sent a shiver down her spine.

"Juden kopf," he was saying. "That woman is a Juden kopf, she has the face of a Jew. I can see that Jew face from here."

Sipora would tell Nardus later in the day, and before nightfall, she would be gone. It was no longer safe to remain here.

THE BOAT

Although the conditions on Boekman's boat had been tolerable for Sipora, after the incident with the Nazi boat, Nardus was convinced it was no longer safe to remain there.

Sipora said her good-byes to the Boekmans. She had been there for about four weeks, and although they had not been the most pleasant people, no harm had come to her, and she had been given enough to eat. They were cold and unpleasant people, but they were not bad people, and for what they had provided her, she owed them the courtesy of at least letting them know that she would be on her way.

Over the course of the past month, through contacts he had made, Nardus had been able to find a place to bring Sipora in the event that she needed to leave in a hurry. The people were farmers by the name of Kruithof. Kruithof was a member of the underground, so there was no question as to the safety of being in his care; however, his neighbors were comprised of not only native Dutchmen but Germans as well. This not only limited the activity that he had in underground activities, it also limited the amount of time Sipora would be able to stay there. The one thing that was good about being at the Kruithof's was that they lived near the polder, making it much easier for Nardus to visit. However, once again, due to the environment, that too required extra caution.

After two weeks, Kruithof had secured what he was confident would be a safer location for Sipora to stay, at least for the time being. He took her to a young couple by the name of Den Olde, a wonderful young couple who treated Sipora with warmth and kindness.

The time at the Den Oldes turned out to be the easiest time Sipora had been through in quite a while. The Kruithofs were very good people and had made her feel comfortable and as safe as possible, but with the amount of Germans living in close proximity, there was no way she could remain there for long.

The Den Oldes lived on the polder as well. The difference between their home and the Kruithof home was that it was a quieter, more secluded farm, and staying out of everyone else's way was not a difficult thing for the family or anyone staying there to do. At least for some period of time.

Sipora did not know this at the time, but her immediate future was already being planned out. There was no rush to get her off of the Den Oldes' farm, but like all the other situations before this one, it was only a matter of time till she would have to pick up and go somewhere else. She knew that; she just didn't know that Spegt was already keeping his eyes open for what would be the next place to take her.

After being moved around to so many places, Sipora was given something in the Den Olde household she had not received for over three years: privacy. With Nardus working on the polder and only a few miles away, he and Sipora were able to spend many nights together, alone in her room. The Den Oldes knew he would visit, knew he was sleeping with Sipora in her room, and did not mind whatsoever. This was something that was so new for Sipora that she had no frame of reference to compare it to. Before Nardus, she had never slept with a man. Now she was sleeping with him on a regular basis. His company was welcome, and being with him gave her a feeling of comfort and safety. It was still difficult for her to reconcile in her head what she was doing, especially when she thought of Hans, but her feelings for Nardus had grown into something much deeper than she had expected. Those feelings were what she tried to focus on during all the nights they spent together.

For Nardus, this was a much more acceptable situation as well. Of course he was happy he had this time alone with Sipora, and he was glad that he was made to feel welcome at this home, but for him, someone always on the lookout for the dangers right around the corner, the two weeks at the Kruithofs followed by these past five weeks at the Den Oldes were so much more acceptable to him than Boekman's boat, that Nardus found himself less concerned on a day-to-day basis.

Sipora made every effort to make herself useful while she stayed there. She learned how to milk cows and help in the birth of baby pigs. These things made her smile and even made it possible to have fun for the first time in a long time.

In times when evil ruled, it was the kindness and decency of certain individuals that gave people that little spark of hope they needed to go to the next stage of their journey. These people are not the most well known of the righteous or heroic, but without that little yet significant role they would play, many lives would have been lost. For Sipora, the Den Oldes would fall into that very special category.

She had no reason to want to leave and was in no hurry to, but the decision was not to be hers. The area was not as safe as it had been, and with more and more Germans entering and patrols increasing on nearby farms, after six weeks, Spegt decided that she needed to be moved to another location, if possible, one that was more permanent than the Den Olde farm.

It was the middle of January, and the weather was cold and windy. Spegt arrived at the Den Oldes at around four o'clock and told Sipora that she needed to be ready in less than an hour. There was a ship leaving from Schokland to the nearby town of Zwolle, and the wheels had been put in motion to get Sipora to the next safest location.

Sipora had not met Spegt before. However, after Nardus had met him, he received enough confirmation of his activities to be as comfortable as he could be with anyone; this was a man with decent intentions. There was no way to be sure, there never was during these desperate times, but Spegt seemed to be as good of a bet as any other, and with the Nazi dragnet closing in on the area, staying anywhere nearby was not a viable option for Sipora. So Nardus told Sipora that when Spegt came for her, she must listen to what he told her and follow him to wherever he would take her.

It was less than a month into the season of winter, and the days were still very short. When they left the farm, total darkness had set it in; Spegt warned Sipora it would be a very difficult night. There was a light rain falling, and with the temperature close to freezing, the drops felt like pellets of ice on Sipora's face.

This was going to be more than just a walk in the field to the next location. It was going to be complicated and dangerous, and Spegt had specific instructions he needed to make clear to Sipora as they started walking from the Den Olde farm.

"Here is how this is going to work," he began in a blunt and strong tone. "When we get to the boat, you are to say nothing. Do not speak to me or to anyone else. There will be a man there. The two of you will board the boat together. You need to act as though the two of you are in love. He already knows what he needs to do and will be ready. You need to be as well. I will be very close the entire time, and I will be prepared to do something if I need to, but you need to do this the way I am telling you to if you want to make it off the boat safely."

Although she did not know what was going on exactly, Sipora knew she had to listen to this man. He was straightforward and a bit cool in his demeanor, but there was something compassionate in his tone, and with Nardus having instructed her to listen to him, Sipora gave him no resistance. At this point, her fear was growing anyway, and she had no other choice but to follow his directions.

When they were within sight of the boat, Sipora saw a good-looking young man waiting off to the side. He glanced briefly at Spegt, and then, with the rain dripping off the rim of his hat, he smiled at Sipora.

"Hi, sweetheart," he said with a smile, going right into the role he was instructed to play. "Time for us to get going."

Sipora forced a smile back at the man. She knew he was on her side, but she was so frightened right now that any show of happiness or pleasure required the utmost effort. She was in the care now of two men she didn't know, had no idea where she was ending up, was wet and cold, and was about to get onto a boat with a very odd appearance. It looked empty, almost deserted. There was one man at the helm while the bulk of the boat behind him was a flat plank of wood. There was clearly room under the deck, and Sipora had the feeling that was where they were going.

Spegt walked ahead of them, now no longer appearing as though he were escorting them. He opened a hatch on the bulkhead of the boat and began to climb down. Sipora and the young man followed behind him. The man went first and extended his hand to Sipora.

They were now in what looked like a large cabin. There were maybe six or seven tables spread around the room, with a few benches evenly distributed around the edges. In a smooth, unassuming fashion, Spegt lay himself down on one of the benches. Following his lead, Sipora and the young man sat on a table near to where Spegt was, smiling at each other. There were a few men on different tables, and there was no way of determining if they were Dutch or German. They all looked comfortable and unafraid, but Sipora knew that it was entirely possible that they were putting on the same performance that she was.

The boat's motor got louder as they pulled away. The trip over the Ijssel River to Zwolle would be about forty-five minutes long. Spegt was lying on the bench facing her and the man, with his hand inside his jacket. The men on the other tables, appearing to be under the influence of alcohol, were getting louder and more rowdy.

"Kiss her already," shouted one toward the man sitting with Sipora.

The young man, cool and composed, turned toward them and laughed. Then he turned to Sipora and gave her a soft kiss on the cheek, managing to appease the shouting man while displaying respect for Sipora at the same time.

Sipora glanced at Spegt. Seeing her fear and concern, he opened his jacket slightly, revealing the hand he had inside it, holding a pistol and ready to be used at a moment's notice. The whole scenario terrified Sipora, but she also knew that Spegt had a clear advantage should something happen here, so in a small way, seeing Spegt's weapon gave her comfort.

As the ride continued, Sipora sat quietly. As Spegt had told her, she sat there saying nothing other than the occasional affectionate response to the man sitting next to her. After about forty minutes, which felt like many hours to Sipora, the boat's motor began to power down and it pulled into a small makeshift port.

They left the boat as they had boarded it. After the rest of the passengers left, Spegt went first, followed by the young man, with Sipora right behind him. As she reached the deck, helped by the young man's hand, Sipora saw Spegt light up a cigarette. Struggling to get it lit in the now steady rain, he managed to do so and get off a few drags. He looked back at Sipora and the young man escorting her off the boat. By now the other passengers were away from the boat, and in the darkness, it was hard to see too far in the distance. The look seemed to be some sort of code.

"Good luck to you," said the young man, and nodding his head toward Spegt, he walked away, his own journey planned out before the boat had left. Sipora would never see this man again and would never know who he was and what would come of him.

"Come," said Spegt. "We'll go to my home first. You can warm up and eat something before we continue on to next stage of the trip."

ONE LAST MOVE

By this time, Sipora had developed an almost complete trust for Spegt. All he done since they had met him was help, and she had no reason to believe that was going to change now. What kind of man risked everything for people he didn't know? This man could have so easily remained out of the war. He was a professor of agriculture in the University of Wageningen before the war began and had no reason to be helping, other than his passion for what was right and a basic love for people. This was a man of goodness, intelligence, but most of all courage.

Spegt had an idea of where he wanted to take Sipora, but in order to get there, they first needed to go to the home of another Resistance operative. This operative would be able to provide them with all the information they needed to proceed. It took a little over an hour to arrive at their destination, but this time it seemed to be worth it. Sipora had not seen anything like this in a very long time. She was standing at the entrance of what was a vast and lush farm, and on this cold and rainy day, a day that was filled with more of the same fear and uncertainty she was growing accustomed to, knowing that this was the home of a friend gave Sipora a warm feeling inside.

As they walked into the home, they were greeted in a hallway by a man in his late thirties. He had a strong yet kind expression. It was evident that he had complete trust in Spegt, because he greeted him in the fashion that one greets someone they have a special relationship with. The smiles and hugs they exchanged were those that in these trying times only existed between two people who had been through the greatest challenges together and had earned each other's trust and affection.

"Tinie," he said, turning to Sipora and using the assumed name she arrived with, "allow me to introduce to you my good friend, Albert Jan Immink."

Sipora, still cold and somewhat afraid of everything she was dealing with, extended her hand and greeted Albert Jan with as much warmth as she could muster.

"You must be cold and hungry," Albert Jan said in a hospitable tone you would expect to be saved for invited guests. "Come inside where it is warm, and my wife Jansje will give you a warm meal."

As she walked with Spegt into the dining and living area, Sipora was amazed at all the activity taking place. She expected to walk in and find a family, but what she found more resembled a hostel. There were mostly men and some women talking, eating, helping in the kitchen, and moving about freely. No one seemed nervous or tense, and it was clear that they were all being fed. Seeing the look of amazement on Sipora's face, Spegt spoke up.

"Albert Jan is a great man. The people he has coming in and out of here are from all parts of Holland. Some are Jewish like yourself, some are regular Dutchmen who have no place to go, some are fugitives; to him it doesn't matter. Anyone who has nothing to do with the Nazis, he and Jansje are happy to help. He gives them fair and honest work in exchange for shelter and food."

"Will I be staying here too?" asked Sipora.

"That's not the plan," replied Spegt. "I want to get you somewhere that there is a chance of keeping you safe for an extended period of time. Most people here are more transient. I have people in mind but we first need to sit and discuss it with Albert Jan."

Jansje Immink put a plate down in front of Sipora and sat next to her husband. Sipora ate, enjoying one of the best meals she had in a long time as the others spoke.

"Jansje's brother lives a little ways from here in a small village," Albert Jan said in a calm, informative tone. "He and his wife have a little boy of about five or six, and she is pregnant with their second child. He and his brother are active with us in the underground and are good people. His brother already has a little Jewish boy living with them; he lives right next door, so they are not afraid to help at all. Besides, they are looking for someone to help around the house. The woman you saw in the other room is Jewish as well, but if she behaves there the way she does here, I won't be doing them any favors," he said, forming a slight grin. "I'll let her stay here and be our problem."

Sipora spoke now. "I have been working as a nurse for over a year and a half, so seeing that the woman is pregnant, it will work out perfectly," she said, taking a break from this wonderful meal given to her by these wonderful people.

"The only bad news," continued Albert Jan, "is that you need to go tonight. They do not know that you are specifically coming tonight, but we have an understanding that for security purposes, anyone we send to them comes at night and is escorted by someone they know."

Albert Jan turned to Spegt. "I will give you both bicycles to make the trip go a little faster. I am sorry but the sooner you get there, the better, and like I said, you must arrive there at night. Take a little time to relax after the meal, but I would advise you to leave as soon as you feel ready."

"No, that makes sense," replied Spegt. Turning to Sipora, he continued, "These are very nice people. You will be safe and well treated by them."

Not questioning the plan but just because she was curious to know, Sipora asked, "So where is it that we are going?"

"To a small town called Lemerlerveld," replied Albert Jan. "To the home of Lubertus and Geeske te Kiefte."

MEETING THE TE KIEFTES

As they turned their bicycles onto the next street, Sipora once again allowed herself to hope that they had finally reached their destination. It was that temperature outside when the precipitation was still rain, but the feeling in the air was like the ice of winter. She and Spegt had been riding for what seemed like an eternity in this cold, driving rain, and had it not been for the remarkable dedication of this man riding with her, Sipora doubted she would have been able to handle this journey.

So when they rode by what looked like a large work shack and he pulled to a stop in front of the home just two doors down, Sipora began to cry in relief. She was wet, cold, and frightened as Spegt knocked on the door with a few special taps that could only have been a code.

The door opened, and standing before Sipora, as she dripped with rain and shivered from the cold, was an enormous figure of a man. He shook Spegt's hand, engulfing it in his own. He then gently put his hand under Sipora's elbow and told them both to come in out of the rain and cold.

"Bertus te Kiefte," he said, shaking Sipora's hand in a manner more gentle than that in which he had shaken Spegt's. "Come and meet Geeske."

Walking in from the other room was a tall, thin woman, a welcoming smile on her face and dish towel in her hands as she spoke in a way that made the whole situation seem so natural. "Here I come. Geeske," she said, extending her hand to Sipora in introduction. "Oh, you are so wet. Let me get you a towel and some dry clothes."

Looking to Spegt, she said, "Sit down, jonge. Bertus will get you a nice cup of tea."

Bertus walked over to the kitchen to prepare the cup of tea for his friend as he threw a towel over to him so he too could dry off.

Bertus looked over at Sipora as she and Geeske walked out of the room. He had tried not to stare but he had never seen an image such as this one. This woman, with this dark hair and complexion, with a face that could only be Jewish, stood there, dripping cold and miserable. And she was so small. This tiny Jewish woman, so wet and cold and sad. Bertus's heart went out to her immediately.

And yet, even in her somewhat tragic and pathetic appearance, she almost had a degree of charm. Bertus, who almost always knew what to do, was at a loss right now as to what to say or do. He was more than happy that Geeske was still awake, for he felt so for this young woman's plight that he was unable to think about anything else.

Spegt, realizing what was going through Bertus's mind, felt this would be a good time to give him a little overview of the situation.

"Minister Vogelaar introduced me to a man in Schokland, a man who had come with her from Amsterdam," explained Spegt. "Her family is gone, and she was working in one of the Jewish hospitals over there until they cleared the whole thing out. They found her a place to hide, and the man came to work in the polder. He too was a Jew but since he looks more like you and me, with his false papers, no one knows that he is. I've gotten word on him from the people in Amsterdam who know him. He likes to fly solo, but he's done some very good things. He has a thing for the girl and kind of comes with the package, if you know what I mean."

"Do you mean he wants to stay here as well?" asked Bertus in a tone that indicated neither approval nor disapproval.

"No," answered Spegt, "he will be either working on the polder or helping with things we ask of him. He's already made clear to me his willingness to help. I would just expect to see him visit from time to time."

"That won't be an issue," said Bertus. "If anything, it will help the woman to have someone she knows come to see her from time to time."

Bertus's tone became more somber.

"Does she know what is happening?" he asked Spegt.

"It's hard to tell," Spegt replied. "The man she is with, he calls himself Jan, seems to be pretty clear as to the Nazis intentions, even if he doesn't actually know the details."

Bertus lowered his head, his tone more somber as he spoke. "From what we are hearing, they are killing them all. Men, women, children, sick, healthy, old, and young. They have special camps set up designed just for the purpose of killing Jews."

"Then what we are doing is even more important," said Spegt in his unwavering tone. "We will save as many as we can."

"She will be safe here," declared Bertus. "There is only one person in the entire village who has shown any support for the German cause, and he's been spoken to by a number of us. If anything were to happen to her or any of the other Jews hiding in the village, he knows it will not end well for him."

Just as he finished his sentence, Bertus watched Geeske and Sipora come back into the living room. Sipora had cleaned up a little and dried off; she was wearing clothes that were too big for her, but dry at least.

"Let me get you both something to eat," said Geeske in that same easygoing, matter-of-fact tone.

Sipora sat quietly. Everything about these people seemed so uncomplicated. It was as though taking care of people was part of their regular day. Still, being that she was in a new place, with people she did not know, she was frightened and uncertain. She began to wonder if this was just the way she would be every time she went somewhere new from now on. The joy she got from hearing Mozart or the pleasure she felt when talking and laughing with friends were once feelings that felt natural to her. Now they had been replaced with trepidation and anxiety. She tried not to think about it, instead choosing to enjoy the fact that she was getting her second good meal in one day. They all sat around the table, with most of the talking being done by Bertus and Spegt. They talked about people Sipora did not know but expected she would meet at some point down the road.

After they finished their dinner and sat for a while, Spegt got up.

"Well, my friends, I need to head back from where I came. There are things to be done and people who will be expecting me," he said in the confident and sturdy manner he seemed to do everything. Looking at

Sipora, he continued, "This is where I take my leave of you. I will see to it that Jan knows where to find you. If everything remains stable, you should be able to remain here for quite some time. There will be no more running. For the time being, at the very least."

Exhausted, scared, but almost awestruck in gratitude for the efforts of the man standing before her, Sipora pushed the words through her lips as the tears welled up in her eyes. "Thank you," she said. "I will never forget what you've done for me."

Spegt just smiled, bid good-bye to the others, and was on his way, leaving Sipora in what was to be her new home.

Bertus and Geeske te Kiefter with son Gerrit

LEMERLERVELD AND A NEW LIFE

The countryside of the Netherlands has always been a beautiful place. The temperate, damp climate allows vegetation to thrive and produces an abundance of greenery. As you drive through the different parts of rural Holland, you will find trees, farm houses, cows, and horses everywhere, and of course the well-known symbol of Dutch culture, the windmill.

It is not at all uncommon to find a little village with one long canal running through it along what most likely will be the major road of the town.

The structure of these villages is usually one in which they belong to the municipality of a nearby city. One such village is the village of Lemerlerveld. Due to its particular geographic placement, Lemerlerveld actually belongs to four different municipalities: Ommen, Zwolle, Deventer, and Lemele.

Lemerlerveld was filled with native Dutch people, with generations of pure Dutch background. The religion of most of the small population being Protestant, many of the people in Lemerlerveld had never met a Jew in their life.

As she finished drying the last of the dishes, Sipora took a moment to reflect on these first few days in Lemerlerveld. She had been so frightened when she had first arrived. Bertus and Geeske were good people, but as is always the case, when people first learn to know each other, there is a feeling-out process that is never easy.

Her first day there had been the most difficult. They had provided her with a room in which she was safe and warm, but when she woke up that first morning in a strange environment, at the mercy of people she did not know, the anxiety she had felt so often in previous days returned.

Geeske was a kind and generous person, but in the beginning she came across quiet and reserved in Sipora's presence. She showed her the way around the house and let her know the tasks she expected her to take on, but beyond that, at least at first, they had very little conversation. Geeske would spend much time attending to her son Gerrit, who was approaching his sixth birthday; he was a good boy but a very active one. Sipora could tell just by the polite manner in which this cute little blond boy spoke to her that these were fine, well-mannered people.

Bertus and Geeske's home was part of a larger structure that included the home of Bertus's brother Gerrit Jan, his wife Tina, and their three children, Gerrit Jan and two daughters, Lies and Aaltje. Also living with them was a Jewish boy named Carly of about seven years old, who had been there for quite some time now.

Separating the two homes was a small area where chickens were housed. Jan, as Bertus's brother was called by most people, lived in the house closer to the work area, where he and Bertus spent much of their day.

Part of what they were doing was building a special room where Sipora would sleep. Bertus and Geeske would continue to let Sipora live there for as long as the situation dictated, but with homes being randomly searched all over Holland at any time, and more often than not at night, it would not remain safe for Sipora to sleep in their home. Although they were comfortable with her being a member of the household, and would treat her with respect and dignity, they still had considerable anxiety when she slept in the house. With his wife four months pregnant, and their young son's childish innocence, which would not allow him to understand the importance of discretion surrounding the woman living there, Bertus knew that it was a risk having Sipora sleep there for too long.

Bertus spent part of the first few days working inside the house. Near the front of the house, in the wall facing Jan's house, was a closet. Bertus knocked down the wall at the back of the closet and built a little room directly behind it. He replaced the back wall of the closet with what appeared to be another wall but was in actuality a trap door leading to the little room he had built as an emergency hiding place.

For the first few days, while things were getting organized and all parties were getting to know each other, Sipora remained in the house. But as Bertus and Jan drew closer to completing her more permanent living quarters, Bertus set up a small area in the shed behind the house, where Sipora would be able to sleep with some degree of comfort.

Unlike the past few years, the days here were normal ones. Sipora had been there for about a week and a half, and although the work was tiring and she was very active for a large part of the time, she felt somewhat better with each passing day. The efforts of cooking and cleaning were far more acceptable and reasonable to her than the agonies she had experienced and witnessed till now in Amsterdam. The situation still felt strange to her, but so far these people had done nothing but feed her well, treat her with respect, and do everything to let her know she was safe. From the almost daily visits by Kryn Hoogeboom, who with his mobile supermarket provided the family with much of the needed essentials, to visits from the local ministers, Keres and Vogelaar, to Gerrit and Carly playing together in the living room, Sipora was starting to feel more at ease than she had in quite some time. The overall situation would remain horrifying and gloomy, but at least the days didn't go by with the constant threat of imminent danger.

Bertus knew that when a Nazi patrol came through the village, whether it was to stop or just use the route to reach another destination, they always traveled by motorized vehicles such as trucks, cars, or motorcycles. Since the war had started, this allowed them some degree of warning. So when there was a knock on the front door and a young thin man walked in, Bertus was more curious than alarmed. Whoever he was, he did not look like someone in need of building supplies, like many of those who did come in, and yet he did not look like someone coming around begging for food and shelter.

"May I help you?" asked Bertus in a confident yet curious tone.

"I am looking for Bertus te Kiefte," replied the man in a commanding yet nonthreatening tone.

"And you are?" answered Bertus, not yet willing to give away information to this complete stranger.

The man paused and gave a very brief yet telling glance at Jan te Kiefte. Catching the look, Bertus said, "It's all right. This is my brother. Anything you need to say to me, you can say to him."

Now more comfortable with the entire situation, the man's entire body seemed to relax as he replied, "My name is Jan Henraat. I was told my friend was staying with you."

Bertus smiled, walked over, and said, "I heard you would be coming. It is a pleasure to meet you."

He extended his hand as he and Nardus shook hands for the very first time. After Bertus introduced him to his brother, he said, "Come, let me bring you to the house. Everyone else is there."

After spending some time in the house getting acquainted with the family, Nardus was looking forward to being alone with Sipora. He had been walking for hours, and although these people were very nice and hospitable, the reason he was there was to see Sipora. He would not tell her, because that was not the type of person he was, but these past few weeks he had missed her often. The work on the polder was intensifying, the weather had gotten colder, and there was nothing to do other than work, eat, and sleep. The only thing keeping him going was the desire he had to be with her.

Sipora saw the gleam in Nardus's blue eyes as he walked in the door; they had not seen each other for weeks. They still referred to each other as friends, but in reality they had already become so much more. Their relationship was now one of total trust, and when they were together, they both felt better. Whether it was the intimacy they would find during those private nights they spent together, or the warm embrace or kind words they shared with each other, they had become the other's reason to still have hope.

These feelings in many ways carried more significance with Sipora than they did with Nardus. Although he would go to great lengths to spend time with her, often at additional risk, he was not one to be focused on sentiment the way Sipora was. Feelings of hopelessness and despair would overtake her with some degree of frequency, while Nardus was fine as long as he kept busy. This didn't mean he was happy, it just meant he was able to control his emotions much easier than Sipora could.

Tonight was special for both of them, because it was the first time they could enjoy this degree of privacy since Sipora had left the JoodseInvalide. Nardus would spend the night and leave at first light. He would say his good-byes to the te Kieftes and leave long before the town was awake. The way things worked at the polder, if he returned at a reasonable hour and went straight to work, his absence would go undetected or be treated with very little concern. This was how it seemed to be there now, but things were starting to change, and he knew that his days working there may soon be over. He would not worry about that now. For now, he would continue with what he was doing and make changes when he had no other choice.

A BEDROOM FOR THE AGES

Whenever someone begins a new period of their life, the first days always feel like they are the most active ones. For Sipora, these first few weeks in Lemerlerveld were no exception. Between getting to know the family, learning the routine, and being introduced to the friendly neighbors, Sipora was already beyond overwhelmed. Had it not been for two factors, she may not have been able to handle all of what was taking place. The first factor was Nardus's visit. Their time together had made her feel somewhat alive again. Knowing that there was someone who cared for her so much and would go to such great lengths to be with her gave her the kind of emotional boost she needed in order to continue.

The second factor, and maybe an even more important one for this moment, was that she began trusting Bertus and Geeske. And why wouldn't she? She had been there for close to two weeks, and by now there was no question in her mind that these people not only wanted her to survive, they wanted her to endure. She had begun to get a glimpse of who these people were. The silence she had noticed when she first arrived was not distrust or trepidation, it was modesty. And Geeske's lack of conversation with her during her first days was not disinterest or haughtiness, she was merely not proficient at small talk. She spoke when she had something worthwhile to say. And as Sipora got to know her, she would find that would be often. It was just that to someone new in her midst, it was a bit more rare.

Meanwhile, much of Bertus's time over the past two weeks had been spent building Sipora's sleeping quarters. Having completed it, he went back to the house so he could take her there and show her the routine they would be going through every night for the immediate and indefinite future. With Jan at work, they would have some cover in case someone stopped by for any reason.

Bertus brought Sipora into a side entrance to the workplace. There in the far back corner was a table with supplies. So far, Sipora saw nothing that resembled a room. Bertus got to the table and moved it to the side with far less effort than Sipora had anticipated. Up against the wall were rows of cement. Bertus removed the bags most toward the middle of the group covering a section of floor that was no more than four feet wide. These bags in the middle were actually bags of sandpaper. He then lifted a piece of wood, exposing a rope which he proceeded to pull, lifting up a panel large enough for a man to go behind. Underneath was a ladder that led underneath the workplace. He climbed down first and then called to Sipora to come down as well.

The memory of this place, while in many ways clear in Sipora's mind, was also in some ways cloudy. The room Bertus built, using what he had at his disposal, was small, dark, and often damp. The room would cause Sipora to live as a claustrophobic her entire life, unable to go into any form of tunnel without panicking. It would cause her to develop illness from the cold dampness, and high levels of water on the floor affected her lungs severely in the future. In many ways, the room would always be a terrifying memory, representing the lack of freedom she had and the persecution she would receive should she ever get caught. Bertus was able to fit one light, one small table, and a bed in this very tight space. She would be alone in this room except for those nights when Nardus would come to visit her, and would not be able to come out until Bertus came for her every morning. Once Sipora was safe in the room he would replace the bags of sand covering the entrance to the room and leave the workplace with an appearance that would not arouse suspicion. Sipora knew that all this was being done to provide the safest situation for her and for the family, but she also knew that every night she would go to sleep, she would not be able to leave this room until Bertus or someone else came for her. Many nights she would lie there in fear, wondering what would happen if Bertus and Geeske would be picked up overnight. She would never get out of this cellar. On those nights, in her mind, she felt as though she was sleeping more in a coffin than a bedroom. And for almost a year and a half she never completely lost this fear.

Although Sipora would remember the specifics of the room in a way that would cause her a degree of panic and even sadness, it also would also be a constant reminder of the amazing behaviors of a family that risked everything they had and did whatever they could in order to provide her with as normal of a life as possible in abnormal times. In many ways, this room would always represent everything, both good and bad, that took place during a time she would never forget.

Aerial view of the te Kiefte home and workplace

Although life had not been normal for Sipora for quite some time now, the days in Lemerlerveld were not only welcome changes from the chaos and foreboding she had been witness to, they also represented the first time she had felt some degree of stability. Not only was she in a home where she was welcomed, but she was also being watched over by most of the people in this village of few people but enormous character.

Sipora learned that there was only one person in the entire village who supported the Nazi cause and wasn't supportive of Jews being in hiding there. This man, a local storekeeper by the name of Schapman, had little to do with the te Kieftes. Bertus, Jan Gerrit, and their underground colleague Oosterwegel had paid two visits to Schapman to discuss the matter with him and to be certain that he was clear on the situation. The first such visit came when Carly came to live with Jan, and the second such visit came on the days following Sipora's arrival. It was made very clear on both occasions that they were very aware of his political views and would not do him any harm or bother him, despite his misguided and cruel philosophies. They wanted nothing to do with him, yet they would let him continue on with his miserable life and let him live in peace, under one condition: that no harm would come to Carly, Sipora, or anyone else in hiding from Nazi persecution in their village. If something were to happen, and there was even the slightest hint that it was as a result of information provided from within the town, they would know it came from him. Specific threats were not made, but it was made clear to him that should this happen, it would not end well for him at all.

This was wartime, and in war we often find that the good get involved regardless of whether or not they are dragged into it. They do this for the sole purpose of helping that which is good in life to prevail and endure. People like Bertus te Kiefte, his brother Jan, Oosterwegel, and countless others in this small Dutch village chose to get involved despite the grave dangers they exposed themselves to. For people such as these, there was more agony in remaining silent, standing and watching, than there was in playing a role in saving lives.

Oosterwegel was another one of those special people that surfaced during these horrific times. A man of relatively comfortable means, he and his wife opened their house to anyone fleeing from the Nazi oppression, similar to the way in which Albert Jan was doing in the countryside. Many of the people to come through their home were members of the Dutch Communist Party, who for political ideological reasons were almost as disdainful to the Nazis as Jews. But it was even more common for mobile members of the Resistance to come through their home. It was well known throughout the Resistance in this part of the Netherlands that Lemerlerveld was a place to find not only food and shelter, but help and support in their covert activities.

The two local ministers, Keres and Vogelaar (the minister Nardus had met in Schokland), were also active in the underground and often visited the Oosterwegel household. Different people would acquire information at different times, and as ministers, they would on occasion receive or overhear information that others would not. Bertus was very close with Keres and Vogelaar as well but received fewer visits. The two ministers did visit often enough, however, for Sipora to get to know them and learn to like them very much.

SKATING

It was the middle of February, and they had been suffering through bitter cold for over a week now. With the temperatures dropping below the freezing mark and remaining there for many days, what had been a flowing stream of water through the canal in front of the house was now a large strip of ice that went on well beyond what the eye could see. For a Dutchman, as uncomfortable as the bitter cold can be, a lasting deep freeze is cause for celebration. It's when the ice skates come out of the closet and people head to the canals to enjoy the national pastime.

About ten o'clock one morning, Geeske walked into the living room, Gerrit by her side, carrying several pairs of ice skates.

"Tinie," she called out to Sipora, "I have a surprise for you."

Not making an effort to guess, Sipora smiled and responded, "What is the surprise?"

"We are going skating on the canal," said Geeske, smiling now as well. "And I mean all three of us. You told me you used to do this at home, and I borrowed some skates from a neighbor. They should fit you."

"Oh, how nice," Sipora said, her voice rising with excitement, knowing she was going to be doing something she had always enjoyed and had not done now for quite some time. It was so good to experience something normal, to go out and do something she had done as a child and had loved so much.

As Sipora began to skate, she stayed close to Geeske and the house; she was feeling a freedom she had not felt in years. She would glance up at Geeske, waiting for her to see her face, and would smile at her in such a way as to say, thank you for giving me this little gift.

With the winter days remaining below the freezing mark, for many days that followed, Sipora went out with Geeske and little Gerrit and enjoyed skating on the canal. During these moments, Sipora would forget where she was and why she was there. The life left behind in Amsterdam, the loved ones lost, maybe forever, and the constant running and hiding were not on her mind when she was on the ice. Instead she felt free and let her mind wander off to a better place.

About the fourth day out on the canal, Sipora heard cars coming from the distance as she skated. Fearful that these were German soldiers coming into the town, she skated over to Geeske. Seeing the fear in Sipora's face, yet showing none in her own, Geeske said, "Don't be afraid. Just continue to skate like normal and keep your head down."

As the convoy, indeed filled with Nazi officers and soldiers, got closer, Sipora continued to skate around the small area, shortening it somewhat in fear of being too far from Geeske. Some of the other town's folk skating slowed up a little and looked up at the approaching convoy, which kept driving right through, not slowing down at all. Sipora's heart was racing now, but the fear dissipated as the convoy passed and the sounds of the vehicles faded into the distance.

Sipora skated up to Geeske, shaking, and with tears welling up in her eyes.

"Let's get you back to the house," Geeske said in a comforting tone. "I'm sorry. This is too dangerous."

After she had been cooped up in Lemerlerveld for a few months, Bertus saw no reason why Sipora couldn't take a trip with him to the nearby town of Helendoorn to visit a friend. Bertus would go see him from time to time to pick up supplies for his shop and would spend a little time talking with him over some coffee and cake.

The home was modest yet pleasant, in a quiet part of the serene town. Sipora wore a scarf on her head, not only to keep warm, but also to bring less attention to herself in what was a new and strange environment. Although she felt somewhat frightened venturing out of town, Sipora trusted Bertus and knew that he would do nothing to put her in harm's way. Bertus made introductions and the host instructed them both to follow him into his shop. They spoke for a while, and then Bertus looked around and picked out what seemed to be some small items like nuts and bolts, nails, screws, all things that were small enough to put into a medium size bag and bring back to his workshop in Lemerlerveld.

"That seems good for now. Thanks," said Bertus as he closed up the bag he had brought with him. "If I need more, I'll come back later."

"Very good, my friend," the man said, looking at Bertus with a friendly smile. "Come inside for some coffee and cake." He looked at Sipora, his smile diminishing, and not saying a word, he motioned for her to come as well.

They walked into the dining room, and after greeting the man's wife, who was now preparing the coffee and cake, they prepared to sit down.

Although a warm drink and a piece of cake seemed like an excellent idea right now, it had been a long time since Sipora and Bertus had stopped, and there was something Sipora needed to do first.

"Excuse me," she said in a very bashful and quiet tone, "could I please use the facilities?"

The woman told her to follow as she took Sipora out of the room and led her toward the back of the house.

As soon as they left the room, the formerly welcoming man changed his expression to one far more serious.

"What's her story?" he asked in a tone that seemed odd to Bertus. He seemed more than inquisitive. There was a tone of annoyance in his voice.

"She fled Amsterdam," he replied. "Same story as so many of the Jews there. Family gone, friends gone, and if not for the help of her friend who helped get her to us, she would likely be dead as well."

The man looked at Bertus with an almost scornful look now.

"Listen to me," he said, the inflection in his voice sounding commanding and confident. "She's a Jew. And Jews are not to be trusted."

Bertus was taken aback, yet his strength and wisdom would not allow him to show it. He looked over at this man who he now felt he had misjudged as someone he was willing to call a friend, and with a strong, firm, yet calm voice, he responded, "Time will tell all. Time will tell."

Bertus would leave knowing two things. This man was not the type of man he wished to associate with any longer, and that it would be too dangerous for Sipora to come with him on any more trips to this town. He would meet with other members of the local resistance to determine if any further action should be taken, but most likely it would be best left alone. There were times that all one could do was hope for the best.

Bertus was as established as anyone could be in times like these. Economies all over Europe were in shambles, and unless you were somehow involved in a business connected to the war effort, it was unlikely you were making a lot of money. If you had a business that generated customers and subsequent income, you were in many ways ahead of the game. Bertus's abilities at building and repair made him one of those rare people.

His workplace was an established entity in the region, and since he was seemingly another Dutchman minding his own business, he was able to run his shop without any significant interference. Other than an occasional visit by German soldiers in need of supplies, nothing out of the ordinary ever took place around his shop.

The Germans had people in every municipality, town, and major city. They were, after all, occupying Holland. However, the smaller the population, the lesser the number of Nazi representatives, and the lower on the totem pole these representatives would be. The people of Lemerlerveld, with almost no exceptions, had no support for the Nazi occupation. This was a town of good people who felt that what was taking place throughout Europe at the hands of the Germans was criminal. They also knew that there were things happening around them in Holland itself that were far worse than they could begin to imagine. There was nothing they could do about that, but at least they would attempt collectively to maintain and run their little village as a symbol of some decency during an indecent time.

Although Bertus had the luxury of not worrying about a constant adversary living within their midst, he did have to remain on the lookout for German soldiers driving through the village. It was not at all rare for Nazi soldiers to pass through town on motorcycles en route to Deventer or Ommen or even ultimately back into Germany. Even though most would drive straight through, there were the occasional few who would stop, creating the need for a constant state of alertness.

For Sipora, this meant that not a day would go by that she did not need to be careful. Being outside was always potentially dangerous. As much as she would have liked to ignore the facts and relax, not acknowledging the realities would have been careless at best.

THE FIGHT

Nardus had a little knowledge of the situation in Lemerlerveld, but Sipora had not been in hiding in the village that long, and Nardus was not close enough to Bertus to get the details about what was happening regularly in the town. He came as often as possible to spend whatever time he could with Sipora.

Although they had gotten to Bertus and Geeske through the proper channels, Nardus was still attempting to size these people up. There was no question that Sipora was as safe here as she had been anywhere since they left Amsterdam. She was being kept very busy on a day-to-day basis with various chores around the house. Geeske was busy as well, and Bertus kept active in his workplace, so it was not as though Sipora was the only one working.

One day, when Nardus arrived in Lemerlerveld, he was extremely tired and hungry. Since he had come there to spend time with Sipora, he would not be so pleased if she had to work. So on this day, after walking fifteen kilometers since daybreak, and after once again escaping a dangerous situation, Nardus was not in the best of moods, and when he arrived at the house, his patience was already running thin. He knew that how he felt would be apparent to everyone, but he was too worn out to care.

Bertus went to answer the knock on the door.

Standing in front of him was a worn-down, somewhat disheveled

Nardus. Looking the way that he did, Bertus knew the man standing before him would be wound very tight.

"Hello Jan. Come in and sit down."

They shook hands and Nardus came in. Sipora was in the kitchen with a mop in her hand, cleaning the floor.

"Hello Sip. How are you?" he asked.

"Okay Nardus. Just a bit busy. Sit and relax and we'll talk soon."

They walked into the living room and sat across from each other. They both sat there quietly for a few minutes. For Nardus, it felt like weeks since he had been able to sit quietly, so he just sat quietly gathering himself. Bertus sat there not knowing exactly what to say to this man. He was not his friend and not his enemy, and the man in front of him hardly looked like someone in the mood to make small talk. So he decided to do nothing more at this point than extend hospitality.

"Would you like a cup of tea and some cake?" he asked Nardus. "You must have traveled a long way."

"I have," he replied. "I've been walking since the sun came up this morning. It's okay, though. It's better to walk all day than to be stuck where I was a few days ago."

"I see. More trouble?" asked Bertus.

"Yes. They picked me up again. I'd rather not talk about it right now, but let's just say it gets worse every time. I've had good fortune till now. Who knows when my good luck will actually run out?

"Fortunately," continued Nardus, "I managed to get away and have had very little opportunity to rest. Wouldn't it be nice if we had a few more hills in this lovely country of ours? It's next to impossible to hide in these flat terrains. But since getting away from this place was relatively easy, it may be that they don't even realize I am gone."

While this conversation was taking place, Nardus would occasionally glance up at Sipora. Even though she was busy cleaning, she would glance back at him and smile. She was happy to see him and looked forward to spending time with him. But first she had to finish what she was doing.

"Let's get you something," said Bertus.

"Tinie, could you please bring us some tea and cake?"

"Yes, sure," she replied. "It will just be a few minutes."

Although Nardus was very pleased that he was about to get something to eat and drink, what he really wanted to do was wash up, rest, and spend time with Sipora. He wanted her to finish up so that she could devote some time to him rather than continue doing chores around the house.

"Where is Geeske?" he asked harshly, the tone in his voice implying that she should have been there doing the work now being done by Sipora.

Bertus was an astute man and had no trouble figuring out what was behind the harshness in Nardus's tone. Bertus was a fair and patient man; however, he did not appreciate this man coming into his home, the home in which he was protecting the woman he came to visit, at the risk of his own family. He also was not at all pleased with having to answer to him about his wife's whereabouts, and was going to make certain that his tone made that abundantly clear.

"Geeske is resting right now," he told Nardus with a forceful tone and harsh stare. "She is pregnant, you know? She needs her rest."

There was no question that the tension was increasing in the room now. No one was exempt from stress during these times, and at this moment, it seemed as though everyone's stress was reaching a zenith.

Sipora was stressed by the apparent conflict brewing between Nardus and Bertus. Bertus was stressed by the aggressiveness Nardus had brought into the house with him. And Nardus was stressed because he just didn't feel well, and therefore it was he who was causing the overall tension in the room, which was why the next thing out of Nardus's mouth was the last thing Bertus wanted to hear.

"Relax," Nardus said in a somewhat lecturing tone. "I just didn't see her here and was wondering why."

"I am relaxed," replied Bertus. "This is after all my home. You seem to have forgotten that."

Nardus said nothing. They looked at each other. Even though they both gave each other a similar strong and determined look, this had nothing to do with establishing power or personal contempt.

Nardus was exhausted and was starting to feel aggravated. He had come all this way and while this man's wife was resting, his woman was mopping the floor and serving them tea and cake.

Although Bertus was calmer than Nardus at this point, he had just about had enough. He knew neither he nor Geeske had done anything wrong and had no intention of allowing anyone to come into his home and tell him how to do things. Geeske had had a rough morning, and like Nardus, his main concern was not for himself, but for the woman he loved.

Sipora walked over with the tea and cake. She placed two servings on the table, smiled at both men, and began to walk back to the kitchen.

"Come sit with us, Sip," said Nardus.

Even though she knew this was the last thing he wanted to hear, Sipora was not finished and replied, "I'm still working. I need to finish the kitchen."

Nardus made a face. He was now clearly annoyed, and the look he gave Bertus was a resounding confirmation of how he felt.

"Now it is my turn to tell you to relax, Jan," Bertus said in a definitive yet somewhat calmer voice, addressing Nardus by the name he knew him as. "She will be done soon. I am sure she does not have much left to get done."

Maybe it was the exhaustion or the pressure built up from the previous weeks, but Bertus's attempt at smoothing things over seemed to cause Nardus to snap. "I don't like this at all," Nardus said in a now angry voice. "I've come a long way to see her and she can't have one minute with me because you have her working like a maid."

He had made every effort to be patient and conciliatory, but now Bertus was angry. He knew Nardus was tired and hungry, but this was not an easy time for anyone, and the help they received from Sipora, as nice as it was, was not proportionate to the risk he was taking having her live there with them. He was putting his family in danger on a daily basis.

Behind closed doors, he and Geeske had discussed this, and there was never even the slightest doubt as to whether they wanted to do this or not. There was no way they had any intention of putting this women into harm's way. She needed their help, and they would continue to give it no matter what would transpire.

Nardus, however, was a different story. He was able to find his own way; he could move about freely, was physically strong and resourceful, and had every opportunity to be safe even without one night's stay in their home. Bertus respected him and understood the stress, but he did not appreciate his tone or the implication. He had no reason to tolerate it and had no intention of doing so. This was going to be handled. But even in anger, Bertus was a gentleman, so therefore this would not be dealt with anywhere near the women.

Bertus stood up and walked over to where Nardus was sitting. He knew that the words he would speak would get the message across to him and that there would be little room for misinterpretation.

"I think you and I need to have a talk right now," Bertus said firmly to Nardus.

Nardus, got up, his face getting red, and replied, "We most certainly do. The workplace?"

"Yes. The workplace," replied Bertus. "Follow me."

Sipora was listening to everything that was going on but was too upset to say a word. She just stood there, watching them leave. This was making her very nervous. She saw the trouble that was brewing here and wanted to do something. What if they hurt each other? What if it became so bad she had to leave? So many things went through her mind. She had felt fear from so many different circumstances already that she thought there were no other ways she could feel it, and yet here she was experiencing a new type of fear. The two men most instrumental in her safety were on the verge of fighting, and there was absolutely nothing she could do about it. She sat down and started to cry.

Bertus and Nardus walked briskly to the workplace, both stomping their feet in angry determination. Nardus went in after Bertus and, with no thought of anything other than the impending confrontation, stormed into the workplace leaving the backdoor open and almost running up into Bertus's face.

"Who do you think you are?" shouted Nardus. "Is this how you take advantage?"

"Who do I think I am? Who do you think you are?" Bertus shouted back. "You come here, know nothing of what is going on, and start barking orders in my home. What gives you that right? As for Tinie, you have a lot of nerve questioning our treatment of her."

"All I know is what I see and hear," continued Nardus, still shouting. "Your wife is sleeping, you are sitting, and Tinie cannot even take a break to drink tea with me. Very convenient situation for you."

"Convenient?" Bertus shouted so loud the walls shook. "You think

I am doing this out of convenience? I think you need to learn some manners."

Nardus walked right up into Bertus's face. "Are you going to try to teach me?"

Bertus grabbed Nardus by the collar. Nardus grabbed him back. Bertus had a distinct size advantage on Nardus and would have been able to throw him right to the ground without much trouble. But he was not looking to hurt this man, he was looking to wake him up. As angry as he was, Bertus still had his wits about him. The same could not be said for Nardus, who pushed Bertus. The problem was that Bertus did not let him go, and they both fell to the floor. As they fell, Nardus hit an open cabinet, cutting his arm. Not deeply enough to slow either down, but deep enough to cause him to bleed.

They both got up and stood in front of each other, seemingly ready to throw punches. Nardus was smaller than Bertus but had no fear and was scrappy. If they were going to fight, he would make sure he would not be the only one getting hurt.

"I bet you wish you could get rid of me, don't you?" said Nardus accusingly.

"Stop," Bertus replied with a markedly different tone. "Listen."

Nardus heard it. It sounded like two motorcycles passing the workplace and coming to a stop.

"Germans," said Bertus. "We need to get back to the house now."

Nardus's face was still red. Bertus knew that this little argument of theirs would have to wait and that they were dealing with life and death now. He needed Nardus to realize this too.

"You need to forget about what's going on between you and me right now if you want your woman to be safe," he told Nardus.

Bertus had not been around Nardus in all the different circumstances thrust upon him during the occupation, so he was not aware of the remarkable control he had when needed, especially in view of what had transpired between them. However, Nardus knew that what was most important at this moment right now was that he and Bertus were on the same page, and in his response he made that immediately clear.

Getting straight to the point, he calmly and confidently asked Bertus, "What's the plan?"

Bertus turned toward Nardus and said, "When we get to the house, you open the door. Invite them in and be courteous. Show no animosity or belligerence toward them. That will only arouse suspicion."

"I am very well aware of that," answered Nardus. "I have had more experience with these bastards than most. Probably including you."

"Anyway, enough of this nonsense," said Bertus. "Follow me."

They got back to the house, carefully negotiating their way through the back yard. As they walked in, they heard a pounding on the door. Bertus looked to Sipora, who was quietly shaking, and motioned her to be quiet, carefully putting his finger to his lips. He motioned to her to come with him. Nardus went to answer the door.

Standing in front of Nardus were two SS soldiers. They were both wearing helmets, were over six feet tall, and looked terribly tired.

"How can I help you?" he asked.

The one on the right removed his helmet and said, "We need water. We have containers and need to fill them up."

"Oh, please come in," Nardus answered as Bertus approached behind him.

"I heard you need water," he said. "Let us take care of this for you in the kitchen."

"This is your house?" he asked Bertus.

"Yes," he replied. "And we are happy to help."

"Who is he?" the soldier asked, looking at Nardus.

"He is my apprentice," Bertus replied. "I am a builder and I need an assistant."

"What happened to his arm?" asked the German.

Bertus looked at Nardus and walked over to the German. He said something so quietly that Nardus could not make it out. When they heard what Bertus was saying, all three started to laugh. The two SS officers were laughing the loudest.

Bertus stopped and said to them, "I better stop. If I wake my wife, she will kill me. She is pregnant with our second child."

"Oh yes, all right then," said the soldier who was clearly the superior and had done all of the talking till now. "Give us our water and we will be on our way."

They took the water from Nardus, who had finished filling up the containers, and said with a chuckle, "Thank you, boy. And good luck. I think you'll need it." The two of them and Bertus once again burst into laughter as they walked out the door.

Bertus and Nardus looked at each other, knowing that they had just dodged a bullet. They also knew they had done so together and by working together and maintaining their composure.

But as the Germans rode away from the house, even though Nardus was relieved, he was also puzzled.

"What did you tell them?" he asked Bertus.

"I told them you were my apprentice and you cut yourself working with me in my workplace," he replied.

"And what were they laughing at?" continued Nardus.

Bertus grinned.

"I told them you were very clumsy and that the last thing you would probably do as my assistant is get them water."

Nardus could not help but smile. It would have been so easy for Bertus to have gotten Nardus out of his life right at this time, but instead, he improvised in such a clever fashion that if these soldiers ever came across Nardus again, he would not even arouse suspicion. It was brilliant.

"Where is Tinie?" he asked.

"I had no time to work with, so I had to put her in the bedroom with Geeske," answered Bertus.

Nardus was completely and utterly astonished now. "You realize what would have happened if they had searched the house?" he asked.

Bertus gazed directly into Nardus's eyes with a look of strength and directness, and with steel in his voice, he said to him, "Yes, I do know. The same thing that would happen on any other day that they would search my house."

Nardus looked up, to the side, down, but not at Bertus. He could not believe what a fool he had been and could not yet look him in the eyes. Finally he stopped, looked right at him, and said, "You're a very good man. You're willing to sacrifice everything just because you know what is right and wrong. I am ashamed of my behavior. I was very wrong to question you."

And then Bertus gave him an answer that was so indicative of his character that it was the very foundation of what was to become a friendship unlike most ever achieve in a lifetime.

"No Jan," he said, "you were right to question me. I would have done the same."

The irony of the fight between Nardus and Bertus was that it took place between two men who knew that they were on the same side. Even when they were angry at each other, to the point that it became physical, the intention of one was only to teach the other a lesson. There was never intent to cause the other any true injury.

However, now that this was out of the way, a bond was forming that was far greater than either could have expected. As they got to know each other, these two men, one from an observant Jewish upbringing in the big city, and the other a builder from a small village in the countryside, came to realize that they shared the same core values, values that revolved around decency and honor, as well as the willingness to protect the innocent and helpless, even if it meant risking death.

Bertus urged Nardus to stay for one more day, as he wanted him to get to know a few of the more important people in Lemerlerveld. Nardus knew that the sooner he got back to Schokland, the better, but he also understood that the people Bertus were introducing him to were people he needed to know.

His first stop was to the Oosterwegel household. Oosterwegel was, in some ways, the most active man in town. Being a man with more means than most others allowed him to open his doors to many that others could not. His home was the closest thing to a headquarters for the Resistance in Lemerlerveld. Information flowed in and out of his house, consistent with the amount of visitors and fugitives he provided shelter to.

The local ministers, Keres and Vogelaar, were next on the list. By now Nardus not only knew that this was the same man he had met in Schokland, but that he also had a role in Sipora ending up here in Lemerlerveld. The role of these two ministers was somewhat different. In some ways, they could be more out in the open than the te Kieftes or Oosterwegels could. The cover of religious counseling allowed them to be more open about their interactions with people in and around the town without arousing suspicion from Nazi patrols. Nardus learned that if he needed to, he could go unannounced to the churches of Ministers Keres and Vogelaar.

Bertus took Nardus to various locations around town, and everywhere they went, he got the same warm and welcoming reaction. This was a very special place filled with many special people. It almost seemed unreal that in these awful times, a place existed with so much goodness. Nardus knew that if there was any hope for a future, that hope rested in this small and somewhat astonishing village.

LEAVING SCHOKLAND

For Nardus, working on the polder, as difficult as it was becoming, was still one of the more tolerable experiences of this war. Between losing his family, seeing the Germans occupy his city and country, running, hiding, and doing anything necessary to defend himself no matter how violent, lifting sand bags and pounding wood pallets into the ground was by far the most acceptable to him. With the relative freedom allowed to him, he was able to wander off on occasion to go visit Sipora or help Spegt or Oosterwegel with underground activities. The missions were limited because the Resistance leaders did not want Nardus to jeopardize his situation on the polder, but whenever the correct elements fell into place, they would call on him to help. Most of the time, that meant meeting up with someone in hiding and bringing them to Lemerlerveld or a nearby town, but on occasion it meant dealing with a more important and sensitive issue, like handling a threat. The most common threat would be a native Dutchman who knew of information and expressed a desire to help the Nazi cause, but it could also mean an appointed official preparing an offensive against the Resistance, or just being in such a vulnerable position that the Resistance needed to take advantage and eliminate him.

So for Nardus, his life at the moment was clear to him. His temporary home was here in Schokland, where he had a regular work schedule, food, and shelter, and in between he would get away to help the Resistance, and as often as possible, sometimes on the same trip, he would visit Sipora. It was not a wonderful existence, but it was manageable for now. As far as everything else was concerned, Nardus chose to push those harsh realities to the back of his mind. He never denied their existence, he just didn't feel he had the luxury of indulging in thoughts of fear or self-pity.

For several days, he worked on a ship docked in port near where most of the team's current efforts were taking place. He and his coworkers were unloading dozens of sandbags from the small craft and getting them over to other workers using it in the nearby swamps. Nardus decided he needed a quick break. He stopped to light up a cigarette. He had begun smoking a while back and was finding it to be more soothing on his nerves than anything else these days. The supply was limited, but given the choice, he would rather have a cigarette right now than a good meal. It just felt better. So he stopped and lit up. It was overcast and chilly, but the air was fresh and the cool feeling of the slight breeze on his face, combined with the pleasure of the cigarette, gave Nardus a feeling of temporary serenity. It was important to grab these moments, and Nardus had done a fairly decent job at learning how.

The activity behind him was furious, but Nardus shut it out as best he could. He took a drag of his cigarette and closed his eyes, only to be startled by a coworker shouting to him from close by, "Jan, watch out!"

It was too late. Nardus turned and opened his eyes just as a sandbag that had gotten away from another coworker was right up in front of his face, too late for him to react, and throwing him onto his back. And as he fell, everything went dark.

Nardus opened his eyes. It felt like it had been hours, but it had actually only been about a minute. He looked up to see three or four men standing him over him. As he sat up, he realized that his head was fine but his back was not. He tried to get up but couldn't. Not only was there no way for him to continue, without help he was going nowhere. The supervisor, a low-level Nazi soldier, saw that the work had been interrupted and shouted, "What's going on over here?"

Nardus tried to respond but was in so much pain he couldn't. He lay back, closing his eyes in agony.

All the other men had gotten back to work, with the exception of one, who shouted back to the supervisor, "We've had an accident over here. This man needs help."

"Well, get him off the boat then and get him to the hospital," replied the supervisor. "We'll figure out what to do with him later."

Nardus didn't like the sound of this at all. The supervision was weak here, and the workers were treated in a far more humane fashion than most people under any type of Nazi authority, but it was clear that they would not allow him to just relax in a hospital till he felt better. If he didn't show immediate signs of improvement, he could have no trouble imagining that they would just ship him off somewhere or shoot him on the spot. Throughout the entire Nazi occupation, Nardus had never waited for the worst to happen. He was not going to start now. He had no choice but to let them take him to the hospital. He could hardly move as they brought a stretcher onto the boat and took him away to the local hospital.

He was treated by the doctors and nurses as soon as he arrived, and he was a very cooperative patient, but he also knew what he had to do, regardless of how he felt. He was now rendered useless by the Nazis and therefore most likely would be killed within days at most should he remain in the hospital. If he stayed there for any extended amount of time, it would become a very perilous situation for him. So he made sure to do the only thing that made sense. He waited till he was well enough to move, and less than a day later he checked himself out of the hospital. He knew his days on the Polder were over and that once again he had escaped almost certain death.

COOKING UP A MIRACLE

Going from one place to another was becoming a normal occurrence for Nardus. Staying in one place for too long was not safe. At one point or another, everyone learned this, but not being one to wait for things to happen, especially bad things, Nardus made his moves when he either sensed there would be trouble or when he received warning.

One might say that living a life with constant moving and displacement was hard, but for Nardus, there was never time for the self-indulgence needed to have those thoughts. Was this the life he had hoped for? Was this the life he had planned? There was no internal debate going on inside of him. Of course this was not the way he had pictured his twenties would play out. But this was how it was. There were many others worse off than he was, and Nardus had an instinctive way of understanding that how he felt meant nothing in the big scheme of things. What mattered was survival. His, Sipora's, and those who needed whatever talents or skills he could provide toward their hopeful survival as well. Self-pity would have been the easy way out. But all that would accomplish would be a paralysis that would likely lead to his demise. And that was something he was not prepared to let happen. At least inasmuch as he had the power to control it. His feelings, concerns, or even agonies were just a small part in a bigger picture. Compared to many others, he was the lucky one. He was still alive and had hope that there would still be a life he could live. For those who were already gone, there was no future. Their lives would never be lived. And even now he knew that to honor and respect their memory, he needed to fight, survive, and if God would spare him and give him the opportunity, live a life of his own.

It was with this frame of mind that Nardus was walking the countryside of Holland. He knew, however, that he needed to put himself in a position of stability soon. If he continued to walk, with no place to call a residence or at least a place to work, he would be caught by Nazi soldiers or the Dutch police. He was not that far from Lemerlerveld now, but he could not stay there for too long without working, and there wasn't anything for him to do there. So his next step was to find somewhere to work and to maybe stay for a while.

It was sometimes difficult to keep track of the days, but Nardus was fairly certain today was a Thursday. Even though it was even harder to gauge the length of a trip, he estimated he had been on foot for a little over two hours when he reached a very large farmhouse, where he planned to check out a possible place to spend some time working and sleeping.

Nardus knocked on the door, knowing that claiming to be a farmhand or manual laborer would be a mistake. It had become somewhat common in Holland for German spies to knock on houses and present themselves as laborers in order to observe any underground activities or, even worse, infiltrate the Resistance. So Nardus decided to try a very different approach.

The door opened, and standing before Nardus was a very large man in overalls, looking more inquisitive than suspicious. Nevertheless, he got straight to the point and asked in a straightforward manner, devoid of any warmth, "Who are you and what can I do for you?"

Being that this was wartime, Nardus was not in the least surprised by the man's tone and was prepared to answer him in a similar, no-nonsense fashion.

"My name is Jan Henraat," Nardus replied. "And I am looking for work."

The man seemed somewhat interested. His face softened and his tone grew more welcoming.

"What kind of work do you do?" he asked.

Almost laughing inside when realizing that he was about to claim to be skilled at something he hardly had any ability to do, Nardus answered, "I'm a cook."

This seemed to be just the right thing to say, because the man's entire posture and expression changed. He stood up straight and smiled.

"God must have sent you to us," he said, the smile getting bigger. "My daughter is getting married in two days, we have thirty people coming, and the cook we had hired a week ago has disappeared. Come inside and we'll discuss the details."

Nardus wasn't sure if he just gotten very lucky or had put himself in an untenable situation. Here was a man who had never prepared a warm meal in his life, putting himself in a position where he had to cook for thirty people. The man took Nardus into the home and introduced him to his wife and his daughter, the future bride.

"The wedding is Saturday afternoon in the local church, and we wish to have the reception here in our home," said the man. "We've also discussed it and wish the meal to be red cabbage and bacon. You know how to make that?"

Knowing that this was not the time to start being overly truthful, even though he was not only being asked to cook for thirty people (thirty more than he had ever cooked for), he was also being asked to cook a meal he had never eaten. Growing up an observant Jew, Nardus was not permitted to eat any pork products, and the thought of doing so was foreign to everything he had been exposed to as a child and young adult. However, this was a time where survival was the priority, and if preparing and even eating bacon would help him, Nardus was comfortable in doing so.

In order to make this work, Nardus needed to get to Lemerlerveld so Geeske and Sipora could instruct him on the preparation of the meal. The family would allow him to spend the night in the barn once he told them that he would leave the next morning, pick up some supplies, and return on Saturday morning in time to get to work. He guaranteed them that they would be very pleased with what he was going to put together for them. In return, they would provide him with a week or two of food and shelter. This would be all Nardus would need till he decided on his next course of action. But first things first, he needed to get to Lemerlerveld and learn how to cook red cabbage and bacon for thirty people.

Although this had all the makings of being an event Nardus would look back and laugh at should he survive the war, right now it was a serious matter. Should he not return and properly prepare the meal, suspicion over who he was would increase the chances of these people reporting him to a patrol should one be in their area. It also provided him with food and shelter for as long as they would allow him to remain there. All he would have to do is prepare the meal for the wedding and get some basic pointers from Sip and Geeske on how to prepare basic dishes should he be required to cook more during the time he was staying there.

When he arrived in Lemerlerveld, Nardus was greeted warmly by everyone this time. What had taken place between Bertus and himself on his last visit seemed to change the entire dynamic. It made sense to him though. These were very tense times, and even though it was clear who was your friend and who was your enemy, it was your friend you would be exposed to on a more regular basis. Exposure to the enemy meant much bigger problems. But in what was the closest thing to a normal day, it was the person who was on your side that you would interact with. That meant every mood you felt would be thrown at them. Joy, sadness, fear, anger were often saved for a few choice individuals in your life. So as strong and fearless as both Nardus and Bertus were, had they expressed their anger toward a Nazi, they would either be in a hard labor camp awaiting death or dead already. Instead, the only thing that happened was a little fight where no one got hurt. And with the way circumstances played out, the foundation was laid for strong mutual respect and friendship.

So this visit was much more pleasant than the last, but this time there was actual work to do. Not the labor Nardus had experienced in the polder, though. This was more like the work Nardus had experienced in the Yeshiva as a boy. Because of the suspicious nature of the Nazis, carrying a paper with writing on it created a suspicion. Should Nardus get searched, rather than seeing a recipe for red cabbage and bacon, the Germans might suspect this as being a message to the Resistance, a code or instructions for some sort of action against their cause. Therefore, Nardus needed to learn everything by heart. So he sat there, listening for hours, as Sipora and Geeske taught him how to cook.

It was late Friday afternoon, and Geeske laughed as the lesson came to an end. Nardus and Sipora laughed along just because the whole situation had a comical feel to it, but nevertheless Nardus wanted to know what was going through Geeske's mind.

"What's so funny?" he asked.

"I was just thinking," replied Geeske, laughing a little harder now. "I think you get it, but I am not going to let you try it out here. I don't know if I want to take the chance."

All three of them laughed as Nardus reassured them that no matter what else happened, the meal would get cooked.

After spending the night with Sipora, Nardus was on his way back to make the meal for the wedding party. Everything he needed was there in the kitchen when he arrived, along with two farmhands to help him with extra work should he need it. He stood in the kitchen and took a deep breath. Nardus wasn't scared, but the uncertainty of the situation made him uncomfortable. He laughed to himself as he thought about how his photographic memory had never served him so well. He got to work and started cooking.

After the meal was over, Nardus, not knowing if the good cheer he heard coming from the living room had anything to do with him, stood in the kitchen and waited. He had cleaned up most of the kitchen and, since he was hungry, decided it was time to eat something. The bride's father had told him that he could help himself to anything he wanted. So Nardus prepared a plate with some of the red cabbage and a piece of the delicious bread they had brought over for the wedding. Just as he sat down, the door flew open and a somewhat drunk but happy man of the house came into the kitchen.

"Jan," he said, "me and my guest are very happy. We were talking about it and want you to know that this was one of the best meals we've ever eaten."

Overcome by emotion and beer, the man walked over to Nardus and gave him a big hug, making him unable to see the look of relief but even more so the look of amusement in Nardus's face.

JUNE 24, 1944: AANTJE

Even though these last few weeks had become a little harder for Sipora, she really didn't mind. With Geeske ready to give birth any day, Sipora took over many of the tasks that Geeske had kept for herself. She had to battle with her to some extent because Geeske was not one to sit back and do nothing, but the closer it got to the day, the less she resisted.

On June 24, Sipora sat in the living room with Geeske as Gerrit played quietly on the floor with his favorite little toy truck. Bertus and Jan were working in the shop, and everything was as peaceful and quiet as it would ever get.

"I'm very tired today," Geeske said, leaning back on the sofa, her very large, pregnant stomach making her appear more uncomfortable today than most days. "I didn't sleep well last night."

Knowing that there was nothing wrong with Geeske but also knowing there was very little she could do to make her more comfortable, Sipora asked, "Want me to make you a cup of tea?"

"I'm not really in the mood for anything," answered Geeske, but as she did, the last word rose in inflection as she grimaced. "Oh, something is happening," she said, a look of confusion on her face, as she wasn't sure whether or not to smile.

Sipora and Geeske sat there for a minute, saying nothing. Geeske stared into space, Sipora stared at Geeske. Both were wondering the same thing: Was it time?

"Oh my," said Geeske, as she fidgeted in discomfort, "I think the baby is coming."

Having discussed this earlier, they both knew what Sipora had to do. "I'll get him," she said, smiling.

She went through the kitchen, out the back of the house, and to the workshop.

Sipora knocked on the door as she pushed it open.

"Yoo-hoo," she called out with a loud but pleasant tone. "Bertus, it's time."

With quick and deliberate speed, Bertus put his tools on the ground.

"Very nice!" he exclaimed. "You stay with her at the house, and I will go get the doctor and Aunt Anna."

Bertus's Aunt Anna was Lemerlerveld's mobile nurse. He went straight to her home, fortunate enough to find her there, and within minutes, they, along with the doctor, returned to the house, where Geeske lay on the bed in the living room; without question, she was in labor.

Three hours later, as word got around the village as to what was taking place, family and neighbors starting coming to the house. Ministers Keres and Vogelaar, Oosterwegel, Jan and his family from next door, and a few more friends were all there as Geeske, with Bertus standing right over her bed, held the baby in her arms and with a big smile on her face said, "Come meet our daughter Aantje."

Sipora started to cry. It was the first time in many years she had cried for something joyous, the birth of Aantje.

By September of 1944, the Allied forces had made such progress against the Nazi aggressors that with a few significant victories, they had it in their grasp to end the war by Christmas. The southern part of Holland was now liberated, and the hope was that with the capture of a series of bridges, most of them over the Rhine River, Allied forces could deal the blow that would result in a swift defeat of German forces. Operation Market Garden, the mission to capture these bridges, began on September 17, 1944. It began well with the capture of the first bridges targeted, but the inability to capture the bridge at Arnhem resulted in the mission's ultimate failure. The series of events that followed led to the Germans cutting off food supplies to most of the northern part of the country. By the time supplies were restored, the damage had already been done, causing what would later be known as the Hunger Winter; 18,000 people would perish from hunger, while almost everyone else would find supplies to be very limited and life even more difficult than it had already been.

The winter of 1944 was harsh and long. The temperatures plummeted to such lows that by November, the canals were frozen and outside activity was limited. For Sipora, sleeping in her underground room, the effects were even more dramatic. The initial precipitation, coupled with the dangerous temperatures, found her sleeping in a cold, damp cellar for many months. With the room being above freezing, and the weather causing extensive ice and snow, the floor of the cellar would continuously fill with water. Bertus made numerous attempts to remove it, but with the limited movements the space allowed, there was not much he could do. And when he was able to remove the water, it just filled up once again. For close to four months, Sipora would sleep in a cold cellar with a foot of water soaking around her bed. The air was stale and uncomfortable, and she was feeling more tired and ill by the day. On the occasions that Nardus would visit, he would make an attempt to clear out some water, but he also came to realize that until the weather improved, there was little to nothing he could do about it either. It remained one of those things that Sipora would have to find a way to tolerate until the natural course of events would allow her to come up from under the ground. But for now, this was her only choice.

CHRISTMAS EVE

It had been close to a year now since Sipora had arrived in Lemerlerveld, and although she hoped and prayed that she would not have to live out her days in the conditions in which she currently found herself, the te Kieftes had been extraordinary in their treatment of her and Nardus, and the people of the village had made her feel as much at home as they were able to under the circumstances.

There was no hatred toward the Jewish people in Lemerlerveld. However, being that the population of the town was mainly Protestant, Jewish practices, customs, and holidays were not part of the life here, and living there meant that Nardus and Sipora could not practice their faith. With the positive treatment they received, they were welcomed by Bertus and Geeske, as well as their family and friends, to celebrate their events and holidays.

So on December 24, 1944, as the German forces had fallen in the south, and the Allies moved closer to what they all hoped would be the end of the brutal occupation of Europe, Nardus and Sipora were invited to join the Christmas Eve dinner and celebration at the Oosterwegels household.

For one night, it felt like all the horror, sadness, and tragedy was frozen in time. The night was a special one. The atmosphere was wonderful. The home was filled with the warm glow of candles and the aroma of a special meal. The guest list was a mix of people from town, Bertus and Geeske with their two children, Bertus's brother with his family, underground activists, Communists, and Nardus and Sipora. Maybe the specter of an impending Allied victory made the evening more special, but the warmth and joy present on this night was something neither Nardus nor Sipora would ever forget.

There are days, events, and situations when the world feels like one place, when people who come from different backgrounds and different beliefs come together under God's watchful eye and show that even with all the force and determination of evil forces, good still survives and, on occasion, even thrives. When the manner in which you worship takes a back seat to the basic fact that you do worship. And all that has happened and will happen doesn't matter for those moments that get frozen in time, bring joy to many, and give everyone the hope that there will be a reason to continue on with life's efforts.

Christmas Eve 1944 in Lemerlerveld, in the Oosterwegel household, was one of those nights, and Sipora and Nardus were glad to be part of it.

THE FALLING OF BOMBS

It was the end of February and the Allied forces had begun to make significant inroads against Nazi forces throughout Europe. What once appeared to be the terrifying specter of eternal Nazi occupation and rule, had now turned into a fierce and bloody battle. It was too soon to be sure how things would turn out, but the mere fact that the tide had turned to where an Allied victory was possible, made everyone in Lemerlerveld hopeful that the Germans would be driven out and that the war would be over soon.

It was a pleasant fall day and Geeske was out in the back of the house working on the garden. She had been pleased with the results. The plants and flowers she had back there were doing very well and with the dry weather today she was able to spend some time on work tending to what was her favorite chore. Gerrit was with Bertus in the workshop today and with Sipora looking after and enjoying time with Aantje, Geeske felt very pleased with how her day was going.

She walked towards the back of the garden and looked at the sky. It was cloudy but the sky was clear today, and she could see far into the distance. It was a pretty sight. She saw the trees aligning the canal, with their leaves blowing in the gentle breeze, and in the distance she saw what looked to her like a flock of birds flying in a very organized but odd pattern. She shrugged her shoulders and knelt down and began once again to work on the soil.

Less than a minute went by as Geeske first heard what sounded like a hum, but then it turned into what sounded like loud cars approaching. She then heard a loud explosion in the distance, followed by another and another. One after another as she saw that what she thought was a flock of birds was really a squadron of airplanes, Allied airplanes, dropping bombs on German ships in the canals. Geeske ran towards the house as the squadron reached over head. Bombs were dropping onto the village now, and the house was shaking, Geeske could not make it back in. She ran towards the shed, hoping that would provide her safe shelter and praying that Sipora and her baby would be okay.

As the bombs started to drop and Sipora realized what was happening she took a scared and crying Aantje into her arms.

"It's okay child, it's okay," she said, comforting Aantje, her focus on the baby stopping her from being more frightened than she otherwise would have been. With the bombs dropping and getting closer and closer the house was shaking. She took Aantje and went under the dining room table. Aantje was crying louder and Sipora was doing her best not to shake too much but the bombs continued to drop and the house continued to shake.

Finally, the squadron flew into the distance and the bombs subsided. A minute later Geeske came running into the house, voice raised to a level uncharacteristic for her and called out, "Is everyone okay?"

Sipora stood in the living room holding a crying but safe Aantje in her arms.

Not even a minute later, Bertus came in holding Gerrit.

"Thank God you are all okay," he said. And with a somewhat excited tone he continued, "Those were not German planes. I think the Allies are getting closer."

All three of the adults looked at each other. Not knowing what to say but knowing almost what the other was thinking they said nothing. Maybe this was almost over. Maybe soon their lives would be normal again.

CAMP ERIKA

Johann Baptist Albin Rauter was an SS police leader during the Nazi occupation in Holland. On March 7 of 1945, after a group of about six Resistance members attempted to hijack a truck full of meat, the convoy carrying Rauter engaged the activists in a brutal firefight. During the ensuing battle, Rauter was severely injured. The operatives escaped the scene. In response to the attack, numerous members of the Resistance were arrested and detained. Some of those arrested were participants in the action, while others fit a close enough description for the Nazis to justify their arrest.

It was less than two hours since the attack, and Nardus was putting as much distance as possible between himself and the town of Woeste Hoeve, where the incident had taken place. He knew this was going to be a difficult day. The Nazis would be swarming the area, and at this point he was not far enough away to feel anything close to safe. There was, however, nothing he could do other than stay on the move, in the hope that he would create enough distance to avoid suspicion. He made it to Apeldoorn and decided that his best chance would be to stay inside the city limits in the hope that he would just blend in. This was not to be.

As much as he had expected there to be activity, Nardus was still taken aback by what he saw in the city. The patrols were swarming all around him. He did his best to remain inconspicuous, but it did not matter. When he turned a corner, two cars filled with SS soldiers screeched to a stop, one just behind him, and one in front. He took his hand out of his pocket, which held the bag of "special" tobacco he had been given by Bertus, and on hearing the command to "Halt," he raised both his hands above his head. One soldier shouted, "Das is eine," meaning "This is one of them," as they took him and threw him into the vehicle.

From there he was driven to the local Nazi headquarters where, after processing, he was thrown into a truck with about twenty other men.

Nardus knew that most of the men in this truck were on the same side as he was, but the problem was he also knew that a common technique of the Nazis would be to plant one or two collaborators in this type of situation, just so that they would be able to gather as much information as possible. So even though he gave off the appearance to those around him as being unfriendly and maybe even a bit hostile, Nardus did not care. This was war, and the more time went on, the clearer it was to him that no one was to be trusted. Certainly not someone he knew for only a few minutes.

The truck was driving to the penal camp in the town of Ommen. The good news was that if he could find a way out, he would not be far from Lemerlerveld. The bad news was, that the camp, now known as Camp Erika, was a brutal labor camp where a large number of prisoners were murdered or forced to do hard labor until their death. This was not going to be good, and Nardus knew that this was not a situation he would be able to wait out. He needed to find a way out.

Conditions were atrocious. The prisoners were given nothing more than bread and water, and there were no facilities available to wash themselves. Every day, Nardus would put on the same clothes he had been arrested in, with the same bag of tobacco always in his right pocket. Many prisoners were taken away, some returning beaten and bruised, while others were beaten right in front of him. For whatever reason, Nardus had escaped that treatment, but he knew that his luck might soon run out.

Always looking for the advantage, Nardus was on the lookout for the slightest indication, the slightest opportunity to escape. Should he find it, he would have to use it, for over the course of the weeks he had been there, numerous prisoners had been executed, first being forced to dig their own graves and then being shot. The system was an odd one though. Perhaps it was the fact that Dutchmen made up a larger percentage of the camp guards, but the atmosphere, although brutal and harsh, was somewhat lackadaisical. This would be Nardus's first indication that there might be a way out.

The other element that might play into Nardus's hand was the fact that often the prisoners would be taken to perform tasks outside the camp. Any manual labor needed to be done in nearby Ommen would be the job of the prisoners of Camp Erika, requiring them to leave in groups of ten to fifteen men.

The Resistance operation in this area of Holland was as clever and cohesive as any of the cells around the country. They had the ability to be available in ways that would not arouse suspicion, even if they were in close proximity of the enemy, and an operative such as Nardus would know how to read the signs when there was Resistance support in the area. So Nardus knew that the horse tied up outside the camp, with the cart of hay attached to the back, was his way out. The Nazis, finding it to be nothing more than an unobtrusive farmer's wagon, paid it no mind. Nardus knew that this was one of the means in which captured operatives would be rescued, and that he needed to find a way to get there. At least three or four times a week, the horse and carriage would be tied against the tree, never getting any attention from the camp guards.

After many weeks, and knowing that he would have to get to the horse and carriage as soon as possible, Nardus was still waiting for the best moment to escape. He hated being there, and he was hungry, tired, unshaven, and dirty, but he knew he needed to find the best time to make his move. Recklessness would lead to his immediate death. That was something of which he was certain.

But on this day, the decision would be made for him. Together with six or seven other prisoners, Nardus was brought to an open dirt area. On the ground at this area were shovels for each one of the prisoners. They were commanded to dig, being told that they would do so until the hole was big enough. They were not told as much, but Nardus knew that he was digging his grave, and he knew that the plan of the guards would be for him to end up in it before the end of the day. Nardus had only a few things working in his favor now, and he needed to utilize them all in a span of a few swift and careful moments.

He knew that after the victims would dig their graves, the guards would wait a number of hours before shooting them. This was so that one extra day of hard labor could be squeezed out of the dying man's body. He also knew that today was one of the days when the horse and carriage was outside the camp. When he had traveled from his barrack to his work detail, he glimpsed it tied to its usual tree. And the last thing he had, the thing Bertus had told him would one day come in handy, was the tobacco in his pocket. It had been there some time, and it was a bit stale, but it was in a bag and had a sweet smell more similar to hemp than ordinary tobacco. Nardus knew it would be valuable, and he hoped that it would give him that one extra edge he would need to get out of there alive.

After digging what Nardus knew was to be his grave, a group of twenty men was rounded up and told they would be going to a site in Ommen to move stones and clean the surrounding area. Nardus, as well as the other prisoners, was exhausted almost to the point of illness, but knowing what he needed to do today gave him a boost of adrenalin that made the work a bit easier. Besides, his mind was not on the work, but on what he needed to do when they returned.

It was late in the day and the sun had gone down, leaving just the residual glow of daylight as they returned to the camp. The horse and carriage was still parked in front, and Nardus lagged toward the back of the group as they reentered the camp. The two soldiers flanking the group were walking and joking, their demeanor very loose, and seemed to be just the right guards to approach. They were all to go to the main area, where in about twenty minutes the prisoners would be lined up, and a group of prisoners would be gathered up for execution. They had no rhyme or reason. They had Nardus and a few others dig the graves, and in walking around the group would most likely pick those who did the digging to be amongst those shot, but they would pick a large group and would include many not part of the earlier preparation.

"Hey," Nardus said in a low but distinct voice to the soldier guarding him in the back. "I have something for you." At which point, he reached into his pocket and handed the bag of tobacco to the soldier.

He held it to his face and sniffed it, said something to the other soldier who followed suit, and smiled, saying to Nardus, "I like this. It will be very welcome later."

"I have more," said Nardus. "If you want me to, I will go back to the barracks and get it. It is under my mattress. All I ask is that you let me go back so I can drink a little water. I feel very dry."

Knowing that they were about to get something they would really enjoy later, the two soldiers agreed. Nardus of course was not going back to the barracks. With darkness starting to settle in, he worked his way out of the camp across to the horse and carriage, and then he crawled under the mound of hay.

Five minutes later, he heard footsteps of someone approaching the carriage. He could tell he got on the horse and felt the horse and carriage begin to pull away.

"No one is watching," he heard a man say. "I saw you come over but waited a few minutes to be certain no one was watching. I will take you back to Lemerlerveld."

Nardus let out a sigh of relief. By the end of the day, he would be clean, fed, and once again with Sipora.

"How do you know where I want to go?" asked Nardus. He wasn't suspicious of the man because he already seemed to know so much already.

"It's me, Joop. Tina and Jan te Kiefte are my aunt and uncle," he said, chuckling softly.

Nardus couldn't believe it. He recognized the voice now and lay there under the hay, smiling.

"Thank you very much," he said. "You saved my life."

"It's my pleasure," he said. "But thank Bertus. He told me where to find you and made me come here every day till I got you."

Nardus could only smile now and think about how happy he was not only to go to see the woman he loved, but to be in the home of people who were as good as any he had ever met. In one day he would go from being guests of the worst man had to offer, to being guests of the best. The allies were getting closer and he had every reason to hope that the Germans would soon be defeated. At this moment, he actually felt happy.

THE WAR ENDS

More and more accounts of Allied victories were reaching Lemerlerveld. Nazi forces had already been defeated in the southern part of Holland and in Russia, and now it seemed like only a matter of time till the Germans were pushed out of the rest of Holland. The battles that were taking place were fierce and getting closer and closer to Lemerlerveld.

Most of the Allied forces responsible for liberating this part of Holland were Canadian, and on April 17, 1945, everyone was ready for what felt like the imminent arrival of friendly troops.

The fighting was getting closer, and although the battle was neither in nor against the residents of Lemerlerveld, Bertus, Jan, and Nardus instructed the women and children to stay in one place and under shelter until they were told it was safe to come out. The major battle taking place was more important than the lives of specific people, and although the Canadians would do everything in their power to keep the Dutch people safe, they had one priority over all others: to neutralize whatever remained of the German war machine in the area.

It was one o'clock and Nardus was getting ready to head out. Bertus and Jan were getting ready to do a sweep of the village, in order to give information to the Canadians should they arrive today as expected, and Nardus was going to Helendoorn to do whatever he could to assist the Canadians from that vantage point. He was one of many activists at this point assisting the Canadian troops, who were more than happy to receive

176

assistance from strong young Dutchmen fighting the same battle as they were.

As prearranged, Nardus left Lemerlerveld wearing the makeshift uniform of Allied supporters, blue clothing with an orange armband. He said good-bye to everyone, adding that he would get back to the village as soon as he possibly could.

For many hours, explosions could be heard from nearby. It was clear when the Canadians came across a cluster of German forces, because the sounds of gunfire and explosions would intensify, and as the sounds got closer, the immediate dangers to the people of Lemerlerveld increased as well.

Being the small village that it was, Lemerlerveld was not going to be a staging ground for intense fighting. Nevertheless, Bertus felt something was not right. It was too quiet. By five o'clock, he felt there was a good chance that the Canadians were not far away; however, he had not seen one German soldier the entire day, and this made him rather anxious. Where were they?

Bertus stood near the canal with his brother, looking in the direction of the bridge less than two miles away in Heidepark. When the time would come, this would be where the Canadians would likely cross, and he and Jan, together with Oosterwegel and others who were closer to the bridge, would be there to greet them and welcome them to the village.

Approaching them from his church was Minister Keres. With fear in his eyes and trepidation in his step, he approached the two te Kiefte brothers.

"I think we have a problem," he said, concern in his voice. "The church doors have been locked from the inside, something we never do, and I am almost certain I heard the sounds of men speaking in German. I think there are Nazi soldiers hiding in there."

Bertus turned to his brother. "Stay here near the women and children. I will go up ahead and tell Oosterwegel. If it gets dark and the Canadians haven't arrived, we will have to either stand guard near the church or storm it. We should be able to get ten or so men together. Of course, the Canadian army would be better equipped to deal with this, especially since we don't even know how many are in there, but we can't go into the night with them there and just hope nothing happens."

The bridge marks the location where Canadian troops and Dutch Resistance entered Lemerlerveld on the day of the liberation

There was no disagreement between brothers. The plan was clear and simple, and the choices were limited. Bertus went to inform the others while Jan stood his ground, advising Minister Keres to remain with him, staying clear of the church until something could be done about the apparent intruders.

About an hour and a half later, when standing now with a group of men, Bertus saw the sight he had so hoped to see throughout the course of this very long day. Coming across the bridge in Heidepark were tanks, Canadian tanks, along with trucks carrying Canadian soldiers and Dutchmen wearing the blue gear and orange armbands.

When they crossed the bridge in Heidepark, less than two miles away from Bertus and Geeske's home, everyone knew that the nightmare was on the verge of coming to an end. As they pulled into Lemerlerveld, the residents of this small village with the enormous heart and astounding courage heard the announcement being blasted out from the lead vehicle. "The German forces have been defeated. You have now been liberated from the occupying force."

People started coming out of their houses, laughing, crying, and hugging each other. The lead vehicle stopped in front of Bertus's group.

Oosterwegel, who spoke English, spoke with the commanding officer to inform him of the situation in the church. They discussed it amongst themselves for a few moments as one officer went back to discuss the matter with the commanders of the tanks behind them and the soldiers in the trucks.

Bertus looked back at the vehicles that had pulled in. Nardus was not on any of them. If he was going to make it back safe, it was not in this group. He was a bit concerned. There was sporadic fighting, some of it fierce, going on all over the area, and casualties were high. He did not have the luxury of thinking about it now, but the fact that his friend was not in this convoy was a definite cause for concern.

Bertus and Oosterwegel were asked to ride with them on the first truck to point out the church and to let them know any details that might be helpful in capturing the German soldiers.

Meanwhile, as they approached the church, some of the Dutchmen, together with the Canadian soldiers, began to instruct the people to get back into their homes. They were liberated, and the war for this town was now over, but there was still a danger present, and until that could be eliminated, they were safer in their homes.

Geeske, Tina, and Sipora had not heard the initial announcement made by the Canadian forces entering the village, but they knew that the sounds they were hearing were the sounds of the approach of friendly forces. The tanks approaching were Canadian tanks. Bertus had told them to expect them

The first half of the battalion drove to the front of the church, while the second half stayed behind the church entrance. Between the tanks and the trucks, there were approximately seventy-five Canadian soldiers ready to deal with the situation in the church. The question now, assuming there were German soldiers in there (something which had not yet been confirmed), was not whether they would get away, but rather how much, if any, damage they would cause to property or human life in the process of being captured.

The Canadians surrounded the church. One of the Canadian officers blasted out through the speaker in German, "Come out with your hands raised above your head. Your comrades have been defeated and you are greatly outnumbered. You cannot win."

They waited. It got extremely quiet as the soldier and tanks stood ready in front of the church. Close enough to see, but out of range of fire, Bertus, Jan, Oosterwegel, and Minister Keres watched and waited along with the others.

The Canadian officer blasted out one last warning as he made motions to his troops to be prepared to storm the church.

Less than a minute later, the doors were opened from the inside and out paraded nineteen German soldiers. Coming out one by one with their hands over their heads, they were taken into custody by the Canadian forces. They searched the church, gathered up all the weapons, and declared the church safe and undamaged, much to the joy of Minister Keres.

Now it was safe for everyone to come out, which they slowly did as the friendly Canadian forces rode away to declare the next village liberated from the Nazi oppressors.

Bertus hugged his brother and Oosterwegel and went to Geeske, who came out holding the baby. Gerrit was holding Sipora's hand.

"It's over," he told them. "The Germans have been defeated."

Sipora felt a joy in her heart she had not felt for many years. They were free. She was free. For Sipora, this meant she no longer had to sleep underground. This meant she would have the opportunity to live once again as a human being.

She felt tremendous joy, as did the rest of them, for what was now happening. But as she looked at Bertus, neither of them could bring a smile to their faces, because one serious question dominated their thoughts at this moment.

Where was Nardus?

Shortly after, riding on a tank with victorious Canadian soldiers, Nardus Groen arrived in Lemerlerveld, looking for the woman he loved and expressing gratitude to Bertus and Geeske te Kiefte, the people who made the next chapter of life possible.

THE NEXT STEP

The four of them sat in the room, not knowing what to say or do. Five years ago, the war had begun in Holland, and during the brutal Nazi occupation approximately 75 percent of Holland's Jewish population had been wiped out. Nardus had met Sipora, fallen in love with her, and helped her find safe havens until this one that had been her home for the past year and a half under the protective shield of Bertus and Geeske.

Now they were here, four people, whose lives had changed forever, sitting together in what was now peace time, wondering what would come next. The only thing that was certain on this day was that Bertus and Geeske would remain together, now with a baby daughter added to their household, and their experiences and actions would be their legacy of almost unwilling greatness. Through all they had done for Nardus, for the village, for countless strangers, but most of all for Sipora, they had maintained an almost simple modesty. They never asked for anything, wanted nothing in return, and only hoped that they would maintain a friendship with Nardus and Sipora, two of the most remarkable people they had ever met. But at this juncture, Nardus and Sipora didn't even know if they would remain together. That was the degree of uncertainty they had on this day, the first day of peace.

Top Row, far right: Bertus and Geeske
Top Row, second from left: Sipora
Bottom Rowe, second from left:Nardus, holding Aantje, with Gerrit to his left

Sipora with Aantje

What they had all witnessed, all in different ways over these past five years would change them and their worlds forever. No decent human being could ever have imagined what had taken place over these past years in Europe. The devastation caused by the Nazi war machine and occupations were like nothing witnessed in history.

Millions were killed all over Europe, many in fighting, but so many more killed by methods of brutality and genocide. Six million Jews were wiped off the planet by this juggernaut of evil. Millions more of different backgrounds and nationalities fell victim to what is very arguably the blackest mark on humanity for all time. The millions of lives lost, ultimately for a cause that would be defeated, were lives seen by many as sacrifices made so that humanity could learn the face of evil and know how to stop it in the future. Either man is too weak, or does not care, but there seems to be little evidence that those lessons gained any traction, as killing is still taking place in no name other than killing itself. And although every life taken by the brutal Nazi occupiers would be its own tragedy, nothing would be the symbol of their brutality more than the Holocaust perpetuated on the Jewish people.

The stories that would come out would be hard for normal human beings to comprehend. For many of the Jews of Holland, the last image of the people taken was of them in the Hollandse Schouwburg. But from there, after what was for most a brief stop in Westerbork, the majority was sent to Auschwitz or Sobibor. It was in these two death camps that roughly 104,000 of Holland's 140,000 Jews were stripped, shaved, starved, beaten, raped, and murdered.

This treatment was what all Jewish populations across Nazi-occupied Europe had to endure. Although the percentage of Jews lost was greater in Holland than in any other country, the numbers that came out of Russia, Poland, and Hungary were just staggering. Over five million Jewish souls were taken from these three countries alone, and the Nazi ideology saw every Jew as the same, so each one was treated with the same brutality and was victim to the same outcome: a murderous death.

For those Jews remaining, the task of rebuilding their lives held challenges far greater than picking up the pieces of their nation's war. As word began to filter out about what had taken place, people would have to deal with the thoughts of their loved ones' torture, the nightmares caused by imagining themselves in the same situation, but most of all the guilt they would feel, although unwarranted, that they survived this catastrophe while their friends and families did not.

For many, the only thing they could do at this time, as the war ended, was to make a break from what they saw as normal, from the life they had lived these past five years, but equally as important, from the life they had lived before it had all happened. Everyone in this room, Nardus and Sipora in particular, knew this would have to be the case in order to at least start in some sort of direction. Bertus and Geeske would remain where they were and continue on in this special village of Lemerlerveld, a village that had shown the greatest good during the world's display of its greatest evil.

Nardus and Sipora would just make the next move, not yet concerned with where it would lead them, other than that it would move them forward, and with some good fortune, maybe in the direction of a new and solid life. Much to the disappointment of Geeske, who would lose her great helper and now wonderful friend, Sipora would go to nearby Helendoorn and find work as a nurse. Bertus wanted to build them a home and have them stay in Lemerlerveld to live as friends in freedom, but Nardus and Sipora chose another direction. Nardus, no longer in the position of the hunted, wanted to do one thing and one thing only: He wanted to fight. Anything that resembled, conspired, assisted, or aided the animals that had destroyed his world and the people in it, he wanted to now hunt. However, with the disciplined character ingrained in him as a child, he wanted to do so in the most moral and legal manner possible. So with the Germans defeated, Nardus joined the Dutch Marine Corps, to join the fight against the one remaining German ally: the Japanese.

A STUNNING REVELATION

With the war in Europe now over, Sipora felt that she needed to make some effort to make a life for herself. Although Geeske wanted her to stay in Lemerlerveld, Sipora wanted to regain her independence; if she stayed at the te Kieftes, she would remain under their protection and guidance. She appreciated all they had done, but for now she needed to do something on her own. So she went to the nearby town of Helendoorn.

Once in Helendoorn, with her nursing background, it did not take Sipora long to find a job in the sanitarium. Illness was all over the place, and nurses were much needed.

For Sipora, working in a hospital far away from Amsterdam, and with the war over, was a bit of an empty and surreal feeling. She had no one left, was nowhere near her home, and yet, here she was, doing what she had been doing in a different environment only two years earlier.

The world was so different now. Her world was so different. She almost felt like she was no longer a Jewish girl from Amsterdam. She was in this small town, and by all accounts she was the only Jew around. On top of that, she realized that what was waiting for her in Amsterdam was more than likely a lot worse than what she had to deal with here. By now, people were getting an idea of the atrocities that had been committed by the Nazis all around Europe; Jewish communities had been almost completely annihilated. It appeared as though, with little exception, it wasn't a question of whether those taken had survived, but more so just a question as to whether someone had been taken. Most Jews in Europe who had been taken from their homes had been murdered in the death camps, and it was appearing more and more as though Amsterdam's Jewish population had been wiped out.

So for now, Helendoorn seemed like as good a place as any for Sipora to be as she attempted to move on with some sort of life. She wasn't sure what that meant, as she had no motivation other than survival, but she hoped that until the time came that she found a direction, she would at least be able to do some good in a hospital.

It was August in Holland, and even though it was the heart of summer, the temperature was still rather moderate. Some years there were hot days in the summer, but temperatures rarely got much higher than the 70s, even in August. It was almost never uncomfortably hot, and this year was no exception.

Things were going fairly well for Sipora, other than the fact that she was feeling very tired and weak for the past few weeks. After all that she had been through, and the unhealthy conditions that she had no choice but to endure, it was no surprise to her that she did not feel 100 percent healthy. The only thing she didn't understand was the rising mound in her stomach. With the way she was feeling, weak and somewhat ill, combined with an unexplainable growth, Sipora felt an anxiety that was rapidly turning into a full-blown fear. What if she had some sort of tumor? What would she do then? She had no choice but to go to the medical director of the institution. Something was wrong, and she needed someone to examine her.

She walked into the director's office, who asked her a series of questions and took a look at Sipora's stomach; he put his hand on it gently to get an idea of what it felt like, sat down in his chair, and leaned back with the beginnings of a smile on his face.

When Sipora was only thirteen, her mother had passed away. Her father was not around all the time, and Emmy, the housekeeper, was only a few years older than Sipora. When the Germans invaded Holland, Sipora was a naïve girl of only eighteen. Even with all the serious experiences Sipora had been through, she still had never had the opportunity to be taught some of the most basic facts of life. So even now, at the age of twenty-three, Sipora was still in many ways a young woman learning about life. It was for this reason that the words that came out of the director's mouth were such a surprise to her.

"There appears to be nothing wrong with you at all," he said happily. "We will need to run a few tests to be certain, but as far as I can see, the reason you are not feeling well, and the reason your stomach is bigger, is because there is a child in there. You're pregnant."

Sipora sat back in her chair, unable to speak. In one instance, everything in her life had changed once again. But at least for once, it did not involve someone being captured or murdered. This time it involved life. The new life she was carrying inside her.

She needed to go back home. Back to Amsterdam and back to the house she had lived in. And she needed to get a letter to Nardus. He needed to know that he was going to be a father.

LIFE CHANGER

Camp Lejeune was more than just an average military base. Being the main Marine base in the eastern part of the United States, it was no picnic, but for Nardus, Marine discipline was a welcome change from the world he had been part of for the previous five years. He wasn't sure what the future held, but for now he enjoyed being in uniform, being away from the devastation in Holland, and being able to walk the streets without having to be on guard at all times for the enemy.

Nardus missed Sipora, but after what they had been through together and the conditions in which they had lived, not being together at this time was not harmful to either one. He didn't know what the future would hold, but the war was over and he believed that he had left her in relative safety. They had both decided that at least for now, they would each go their separate ways. And then the letter came.

Sipora was pregnant. It wasn't a complete shock to Nardus, with the amount of nights they had spent together, but it was not what he expected to read either. He smiled as he read her letter. The young naiveté in her written words expressed her amazement at what had happened. She didn't reveal how she felt about having a child on the way, and Nardus's first feelings were unclear even to himself, but there was a great deal of affection between the two of them. She told him how she now loved him and was so grateful he had stayed with her and helped her through what was the hardest time anyone would go through, and yet she did not push any responsibility of the child on him. The letter was to let him know that which he had every right to know: that she was expecting his child.

When a man learns that he has a child on the way, nothing reveals more about what this really means to him than his initial reaction. Some panic, some jump for joy, others get angry or feel smothered. Starting to get his senses together, Nardus had a different reaction. He felt pleased, settled, and calm. Being a man who still had his inherent faith in God and the concept of fate and destiny, Nardus felt at ease with the fact that the woman he had loved for these past three years would give birth to his child.

Nardus was a conservative man by nature and felt no need to run around drinking and looking for the company of numerous women. So the news did not put any crimp in his lifestyle.

He would take care of this child. That was one thing he knew for certain. He made no assumptions that Sipora even wanted to remain involved with him. The letter was nothing but warm and affectionate, but it gave Nardus no indication about how she felt about him. In his estimation, there was no way to know what would happen between them until they spent time together once again. Based on his tour of duty, they might not get to see each other again before their child was born. The thought made Nardus smile. He was going to be a father. The situation was complicated, but after what they had been through the past five years in Holland, most situations were complicated.

Lying on his bunk bed, Nardus started considering all the possibilities. From time to time, his mind would wander to what was lost and how his world as well as the world of the few survivors he knew of had changed forever.

He was shaken into a state of alertness when he heard his name called in a loud, clear voice.

"Groen!" shouted the staff sergeant. "You have a phone call."

There were a few people who knew he was there, but not many had the means to call him, so when he picked up the phone and heard Jacques Baruch's voice, he was not surprised.

"Nardus," said Jacques, revealing the pleasure he felt in speaking to his brother-in-law and one of his closest friends, "how are you, *jonge?*"

Nardus as a Marine in 1945

"I'm okay," replied Nardus. "It's hard work here but compared to what was going on there, I have nothing to complain about. I know I will have food, I know where I will sleep, and to walk freely is something none of us will ever take for granted again. How are you over there? Who have you seen?"

"Fie and I are back in Amsterdam," replied Jacques. "Every day is difficult, living in a place that needs to be rebuilt as this place does, but it is still home, and I am grateful that I at least can be here. But there is much work to do to try to get everyone's life back on track."

Nardus listened as he spoke. This was typical Jacques. Even having suffered the same devastation as so many others, he still was talking about getting everyone's life "back on track." Somehow, Nardus knew that if there was anyone who could have the sort of impact that the surviving Jews of Holland needed, Jacques was that man. They spoke for another five minutes, covering as many details as possible. They spoke of their brother David, who moved to Palestine with Martha and Thea and how Meyer and Roe were (at the moment, at least) in Amsterdam as well. The confirmation of the murder of over 100,000 of Holland's Jewish population was becoming more and more solid. As stories of what the Nazis had done all over Europe were filtering through, it became harder and harder to comprehend what had taken place. The numbers were staggering. Jacques and Nardus spoke of it for a brief moment, but they found it too difficult to speak of and continued discussing the people closest to them who had survived the war.

This had been a wonderful diversion for Nardus, and he felt at least somewhat fortunate to have a friend and relative such as Jacques Baruch still around and able to communicate with. But now it was time to say good-bye. Jacques had reached his limit for this phone call and told Nardus he'd get back to him soon. There was just one more thing Nardus needed to say to Jacques before they hung up.

"Jacques," said Nardus just as he was ready to hang up, "there is one thing I need you to do for me."

These past few weeks, living on Boiler Street in her old home, were very difficult ones for Sipora. The entire time she was there, it was becoming more and more apparent that Emmy was not going to relinquish control of the house. With her father and Bram confirmed to be dead, Emmy appeared to turn colder and colder toward Sipora with each passing day. She showed little sadness when mentioning Sipora's father and became more and more comfortable in the home. Her language was getting more and more clear as she let Sipora know that this was now her home and that she had no intention of returning it to the family that had lived there less than three years earlier. Sipora was told that she was now a guest in her own home, and that her welcome would not last much longer.

When Marcel Rodrigues left the home in what turned out to be a failed attempt to escape, he had told Emmy that should he not return, she would be in charge of the home. Sipora tried not to think about this in too much detail. Each level she peeled away made this harder and harder to bear. She was alone and pregnant, most of her friends and family were murdered, and here she was in what should have been her home, being told she could not stay much longer by the very woman who once treated her like a friend. Now she wondered if Emmy had tipped off the Nazis on where to find her father and brother. It was an awful thought, but this was very convenient for Emmy, too much so, and as hard as she tried to convince herself this wasn't the case, she couldn't shake the feeling.

She had just met with someone who had expressed interest in purchasing the piano once played by her mother and now sitting in the living room. She hated to do this, but with the money she would make, she would be able to get by on her own at least for a short while.

Suddenly, a motorbike pulled up to the house. On the bike were two young men. The man in front had a familiar look about him, but Sipora couldn't place why right away. The man on the back of the bike spoke first.

"Are you Sipora Rodrigues?" he asked in a friendly tone, accompanied by a smile.

Sipora was somewhat startled but felt at ease with the man's approach and confirmed with no reluctance that she was.

"I have a message for you from Nardus," continued the man. "He said he got your letter and that you will be hearing from him again very soon."

Sipora felt a warm feeling come over her. It would have been easy for Nardus to avoid the whole situation if he had so desired. In these postwar times, with thousands of miles separating them, even with a child on the way, it would have taken very little effort on Nardus's part to have no involvement whatsoever with her or the child. She was not surprised, because everything he had done till now showed that the kind of man he was made this reaction more likely, but still, this extra effort meant a lot to her. She was curious about these men now.

"So I know Nardus told you how to find me," said Sipora, "but may I ask, who are you?"

"I'm Meyer Groen," said the man riding the bike. "Nardus's older brother."

Then the man on the back of the bike spoke again.

"I'm their brother-in-law," he said, motioning to Meyer. "My name is Jacques Baruch. It was good to meet you."

Somewhat in shock over having met two people so significant in Nardus's life, Sipora just stood there, smiling.

Jacques got back on the bike, and after the two bid farewell to Sipora, she heard him say to Meyer, "Nardus did pretty well for himself."

Sipora watched as the two rode away. In a world where so little good was happening, this was a day when she could at least smile and feel a little less alone.

NOVEMBER 2, 1945: MARCEL

With the money she had made from the sale of the piano, Sipora could pay for admission to the hospital when it was time for her to give birth. The day had arrived and the labor started, and Sipora found herself in the unenviable position of having to get herself to the hospital. She went to Santa Anna's Pavilion, a Catholic institution not far from where she lived.

By this time, she not only knew that Nardus was going to support her and the child, she had heard how pleased he was with the events that were transpiring. He was still in America, stationed as a Dutch Marine attached to the US Marine Corps, but when he had the chance, he would be there to see Sipora and child. Today, however, he was not able to be there.

After the birth of her son, the miracle that so often looked like it would never ever happen, Sipora gave the little baby two names: Marcel, after her father, the man to give her life, and Lubertus, after Bertus te Kiefte, who, other than Nardus, was the man most instrumental in helping her to keep that life.

Marcel Lubertus had been created by Sipora and the man who empowered her, saved her from death's grasp, and loved her even through times when love was so overshadowed by death and evil.

The circumstances were less than ideal, and their lives were filled with questions yet to be answered, but as Sipora lay there with Marcel in her arms, it almost felt like God was making a statement, a statement that even with the forces of evil at their most powerful, good will survive, love will prevail, and life would go on.

When Thea had been born to David and Martha Groen, it was a symbol of life in the midst of horror and devastation; the symbol held a beauty and power that made it unique. When Marcel came into the world, he would be a symbol of even greater significance.

What was once the bright light of a great world of Dutch and European Jewry had been diminished to a mere glimmer, and a strong powerful fire of life had been reduced in so many places to mere ashes. And now despite all of that, there remained hope. The flickering light of what remained in Nardus Groen and Sipora Rodrigues's life had now turned into this bright, new, and strong flame. The light that was their son Marcel.

This significance would carry a burden, but it would carry an even greater importance and virtue. It would take an almost extinguished light, an almost destroyed world, and turn it into a strong flame, building not one but many new worlds in the years to come.

On this day, as Sipora looked at her son, it did not matter that Nardus was not here. It would not have even mattered anymore if she had been here. What only mattered today was that this baby was here. And whether she was right or wrong for feeling this way, Sipora felt like this was the reason she had survived, and this would now be her reason for wanting to survive.

When Nardus's name was called out, having paid attention to the calendar and having counted the months, he knew what this call was about. He almost wanted to laugh out loud as he walked to the phone. He had been imprisoned by the Nazis, chased, and injured; he had even had to dig his own grave on one occasion, and yet, he was never as nervous as he was right now, as he walked to take his phone call. This was different. This wasn't just about the moment. This was about the future. This was everything right here. With all the challenges he had faced in the war, the end result was simple: survive and move on. But if he was to be a father, he now had the responsibility of thinking about tomorrow, not just for him but for what was to be his family. He had gotten used to living for the moment, without concern for the future. And this time in the Marines had been wonderful for him. It allowed him to live that life without the constant threat of danger and exposure to death and devastation. The structure and discipline were not only a nonissue for him, they were something he had enjoyed.

However, Nardus had been raised with a value system that had shown him what in life held true meaning, and although his personality and character would on occasion lead him to be flawed in the pursuit and execution of this value system, the strength of his character and the core of his being would steer him the direction of what would be not only the right thing to do, but the things that would provide him with the most satisfying and meaningful life.

That all started today, when he picked up the phone and found out he was a father, when he heard the news that he now had a son.

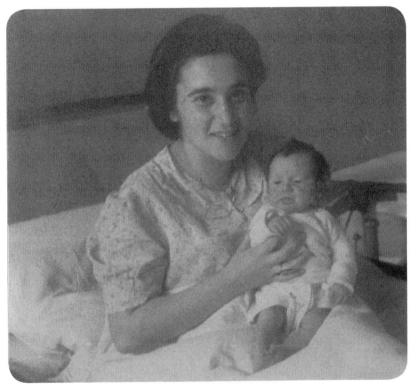

Sipora and Marcel on the day of his birth

In the 1940s in Holland, when a woman gave birth to a child, she was required to stay in the hospital for ten days. This could have been a problem for Sipora, because it meant that life would be difficult financially once she left the hospital to care for herself and the baby, had it not been for one other special arrival on November 2.

Knowing approximately when the baby was due, Nardus had spent most of his earnings from the Marines and put together two boxes of clothes and household supplies for Sipora and the baby, as well as some additional cash as well. It was becoming more and more apparent to Sipora now that she was not going to be in this alone. She was not certain of what her relationship with Nardus would be, but she now knew he accepted and embraced the arrival of this child and would be there to help them.

Mid-November in Holland can be damp and cold, and this year was no exception. Sipora, who had little to no experience in the care for little children, was told to expect the baby to cry a lot, but to let him do so. But upon bringing him home, Marcel would cry so much that she needed to go to him, and she found that he was often so cold that she would have to bring him into the bed with her to warm him up.

Meanwhile, Sipora was still feeling very weak. On top of that, her appetite was poor and she found herself getting thinner and thinner. She tried not to think about it too much, but she was concerned for her health.

In January, Nardus arrived back from the United States to see Sipora for the first time since soon after the war ended and to meet his son Marcel for the very first time. He was warm and affectionate with both and seemed to go right into a family mode. Not being the sentimental type, Nardus never came right out and made any declaration of what was to be. He just came back, went straight to Sipora and Marcel, and acted as though he was visiting his wife and child. He made it clear that was how he wanted it to be, which was what Sipora wanted as well. The start of their life together was not the most romantic of beginnings, but it was without doubt and based on love and respect.

Before returning to the Marines, Nardus noticed Sipora was not well but hoped it was just fatigue; he knew there was nothing he could do about it anyway. Jan Van de Berg was not far, Jacques Baruch could be reached whenever needed, and Sipora could move about freely, so if she needed help, she would be able to get it.

In March, thin, weak, and feverish, Sipora was diagnosed with the beginning stages of pleurisy. Marcel went to the Van de Bergs, and Sipora was admitted to the *Joodse Invalide,* which had been converted into a hospital. Many of the patients there were young women such as herself. Being that there was a concern of her being contagious, Sipora was put in isolation.

Once again she found herself in rough times. She had finally experienced joy with the birth of her child, she was looking to build some sort of life when Nardus was done with the Marines, and now, just as it appeared as though things would be okay, here she was, lying alone in a bed in the *Joodse Invalide*, sick, unable to even see her son. How much more could one woman endure? All the hope she had felt upon the birth of Marcel had now turned into that familiar feeling of despair. She wondered if she would ever get the opportunity to live a normal life. She was too tired and too ill to even dream of the future. So she just lay in her hospital bed waiting to see if was to get better or if this was the end. The only thing pushing her was the wish to hold her son once again. Maybe that would be enough.

The one advantage Sipora had was that with the war over, the medical care had improved significantly enough that she soon got better. By mid-July, she was transferred to a convalescent facility in Gelderland, where she remained until September, when she was released. By now Nardus had completed the necessary studies he needed to be appointed a rabbi in Holland, and by the end of 1947, after receiving ordination by Chief Rabbi Tal, Nardus was appointed to head up the Jewish community in the town of Apeldoorn.

A RETURN TO NORMALCY

It had only been two year since Marcel had been born, so the process was, in some ways, very similar, but for Sipora, on the verge of giving birth to their second child, the most important things were very different.

She would have this child in Amsterdam; she would remain in the hospital for ten days; and she would, when those ten days were up, be picked up by a Van de Berg. One thing was the same: she again had a baby boy.

However, it was almost only the differences, and yes this time the positive differences, that made the birth of this second child so special.

This time, Sipora was not alone. Nardus and she were together; they had been married. There was not the uncertainty of whether or not she would raise the baby alone.

They would name their newborn son Leo, a more modern derivative of Leendert, the name of Nardus's late father. Eliezer was Leendert's Hebrew name and would be Leo's as well.

Having been appointed to head up the Jewish community in Apeldoorn, now Rabbi Nardus Groen lived there with his two children and loving wife, Sipora. Life would oftentimes be far from easy, there would be some serious struggles, and people would still get sick, some would die at young ages, and some would perish in accidents, but the murdering was over. What would happen from this time forth would be the normal things that happen in life; it was no longer that prolonged state in which people asked themselves, why? Why would God just let this happen? Why would people hate others so much that they would want to obliterate any remnant of their existence? And why did I need to live through something like that?

There were no solid black-and-white answers to any of those questions, but the truth was that on January 5, 1948, on the day Leo Groen was born, those questions, although they would stay with Nardus and Sipora forever, were not relevant to the more immediate task at hand, which was the task of building a new life and raising a family. And since they had been spared, they had the opportunity to do so. In a way, by doing this, they would give honor to the memory of all those who had not been as fortunate.

Much of their life from this moment on was still going to be very difficult, but at least it was to be a more normal life, one filled with joys and sadnesses, and the building of a new family and new world.

EPILOGUE

As had become the family's custom, Passover of 2005 was celebrated in Marcel & Bernice's home just outside of Philadelphia, Pennsylvania. Nardus sat at the head of the Seder with Sipora by his side, as she had been now for the past sixty years. He looked around at what they had built together as he recalled how they had gotten to this wonderful dinner.

After Leo was born, Nardus moved his family to Apeldoorn. It was a small community, but it was a strong one in comparison to so many others around the country. While living there, Sipora became pregnant again. Although they loved their two boys, they wondered if they would maybe now have a daughter. However, upon the birth of a third straight son, they chose to name him Ruben, the name that translates from the Hebrew "*Reuven*," for "they saw a son."

In the mid-1950s, Nardus was appointed as chief rabbi for the Dutch territory of Suriname. In the northern part of South America, Suriname has a brutally hot and humid tropical climate. For the three boys, it was far more tolerable than it was for Nardus and Sipora, yet they had been through so much worse than humidity and mosquitoes; for the most part, they were not at all unhappy with their life there, as long as it was to be more temporary than permanent.

With the Soviet Union now flexing its muscles and controlling Eastern Europe, the cold war between the ruling Soviet government and the West had reached full force. For Nardus and Sipora, the thought of returning to Holland, with the fear of another war or occupation hanging over their heads, was somewhere between unappealing and unacceptable. They remained in Suriname and waited for the opportunity to move to the United States.

Their chance came when Professor Jacob Marcus of Hebrew Union College, the institute of higher learning for Reform Judaism in Cincinnati, Ohio, paid a visit to Suriname. The purpose of his visit was to retrieve archives of the history of Jews in Suriname and how it related to the Jews in Holland. The retrieval of these archives required the assistance of Surinam's Jewish leader, a very intrigued and subsequently helpful Nardus. Upon completing his assignment in Suriname, Professor Marcus offered to sponsor Nardus's residency in America, making it possible for the entire family to move. In 1955, Nardus and Sipora, with their three sons, Marcel, Leo, and Ruben, moved to Cincinnati, beginning the newest era of their lives, the life in America.

In the mid-1950s, Cincinnati had a booming Jewish community. Besides Professor Marcus and the Hebrew Union College, Cincinnati was also the home of Rabbi Eliezer Silver, the head of Agudah North America, the administrative and political organization of the Orthodox movement. Rabbi Silver was recognized as being one of the greatest Orthodox rabbis alive at the time. For Nardus, despite the close personal friendship he established with Professor Marcus, the philosophy and lifestyle of Rabbi Silver was more in line with what he had known his life, and he welcomed the opportunity to study under this incredible Jewish mind and intellect. His studies would gain him an additional Rabbinical certification from Rabbi Silver and an even more advanced knowledge and understanding of Jewish law.

Even with his studies with Rabbi Silver, Nardus was exposed to more liberal practices; his friendship with Rabbi Goldfeder and occasional attendance of his local Conservative synagogue made the Groen household a more lenient one when it came to observance. And although Sipora was always learning more and more from Nardus, her less than religious upbringing still influenced her way of thinking, which in turn influenced their lifestyle.

Sipora cherished the role of wife and mother. The work involved in maintaining the household and caring for the boys was far from easy, but it was a labor of love and one she was grateful for. The three boys were growing up and keeping her very busy, and in early 1957, she learned that once again she was expecting a child.

On September 30, 1957, the one element to their family that eluded them till now finally transpired. They became the parents of a baby girl. After first having three boys, they took no chances and named the girl Deborah Miriam, after Sipora and Nardus's mothers, respectively.

They remained in Cincinnati until 1963; while there, they had what would be their fifth and final child, David, on January 2, 1962.

Upon leaving Cincinnati, Nardus took a Rabbinical position in Lansdale, Pennsylvania, where the family remained for about a year and a half. After that, they lived in Margate, New Jersey, just outside of Atlantic City, and they made an unsuccessful attempt at moving back to Holland before settling in Philadelphia for seven years.

In 1974, they received a phone call from Holland, telling them that Nardus's brother David had been killed in an automobile accident. The subsequent trip to Holland, followed by another less than a year later, led them to discussions with Nardus's brother Meyer, who, being an active member of Holland's Jewish community, helped Nardus and Sipora return to Holland. With the three older boys grown and Debby in college, they moved to Holland with their youngest son David in May of 1976.

They lived in Holland and eventually moved to Zandvoort, the beach resort where David and Martha spent so many years after the war. While living there they would purchase a home in Boynton Beach, Florida where they would spend the colder months of the year. As the years and their ages progressed they made the decision to sell their home in Zandvoort and permanently move to Boynton Beach where they would live until purchasing a new home in Delray Beach.

Sitting at this table filled with friends and family, Nardus and Sipora Groen would always acknowledge their good fortune in being able to live a life and rebuild from the ashes of death and destruction. For many survivors a way of dealing with the pain of what took place during the war would be by attempting to never speak of it. For Nardus and Sipora it was just the opposite. They found whatever solace they could throughout their lives in openly sharing their experiences, remembering not only those they lost but the loss of all 6 million Jews killed by Nazi Germany. They would maintain a special lifelong friendship with Bertus and Geeske te Kiefte and speak openly and often of their righteousness.

As they sat here now in Marcel's home, celebrating the holiday commemorating the Jewish people being freed from slavery, they knew that since 1945 they had been given that very blessing. The blessing of freedom.

Nardus and Sipora in Lansdale, Pa. in 1963

Sipora and Geeske in 2001

Nardus and Geeske in 2001

Nardus and Sipora at one of their grandchildren's wedding

IN MY OWN WORDS

I arrived in Florida on Friday June 8, 2007, and was picked up at the airport by my brother Leo. With my father's condition showing little sign of improvement, my mother remained in the hospital by his side.

In the car from the airport, Leo filled me in on what had transpired, telling me that the situation was bleak. Dad's blood pressure was reasonable and his fever had even improved, but with what had transpired till now, it appeared as though his organs were on the verge of shutting down. There was a particular concern for his kidney function, because once those shut down, the chances of recovery would be next to impossible.

When we arrived in the hospital, we received the news we had been dreading to hear. His kidneys were no longer functioning, his body was shutting down, and even if he survived, he would be in a vegetative state until his heart gave out. In essence, although he was still alive, his life was over.

Later that day, they removed him from life support.

Maybe it was the trauma of seeing my father in this condition and knowing that, unless a miracle occurred, I was on the verge of losing him, but that night while sleeping in the hospital, I took ill. My fever rose to 103, and I lay on the couch of the waiting room and did my very best to rest. The fever, clearly caused by the stress of the previous day, was gone when I awoke.

The nurse told us that most patients taken off life support passed quietly within twenty-four to forty-eight hours. She also said something rather curious. She said that often a patient, even on the verge of death, and with almost no strength left in the body, would wait to pass on, either for someone important to arrive, or for someone to leave. I knew then that I could still catch the flight I was scheduled to take the following night. Having looked after me, shielded me, and protected me my entire life, I felt my father would not want me there when the time came, and with Debby arriving the next morning and Leo and mother already there, he would not die alone.

Sunday afternoon, I went into his room, my mother by his side. I looked at her and asked if I could be alone with him to say good-bye.

My father lay there breathing faintly, eyes closed, with very little life left in him. I kissed him on his forehead and said, "You don't have to worry about me anymore. I will be fine." And then something happened I will never forget. With what looked like a man who was accessing all his strength left in his body, my father's eyes opened wide and looked right into mine, almost as if he were telling me to be strong, to live my life correctly, and that he loved me very much. Then his eyes closed, and I said good-bye to my father.

Remarkably, his heart kept beating for almost three more days. Then, on Wednesday morning, on June 13, 2007, his heart stopped, and my father passed away.

Nardus Groen died of natural causes in Boynton Beach, Florida, at the age of eighty-seven. He left behind five children, twelve grandchildren, four great-grandchildren, and a loving wife, Sipora, with whom he had lived for the past sixty years.

Nardus Groen died at peace, with dignity, and as a free man.

ABOUT THE AUTHOR

David Groen has taken his extensive knowledge of Jewish history and combined it with information gathered by friends and relatives in the story from both the United States and the Netherlands. His unique style combines the important documentation of critical historical events with a heartfelt storytelling technique that reads like a historical novel.

As the youngest child of the book's main subjects, Nardus and Sipora Groen, David has had the benefit of a lifetime of the accounts of the events that took place and the access needed for more specific and detailed information gathering. His passionate desire to let the world know the most significant events to take place in the lives of his parents, specifically between 1940 and 1945 in Nazi-occupied Holland, translates into a sometimes thrilling and often emotional literary experience.

David currently resides in Queens, New York, where he has lived since 1987. He was born in Cincinnati, Ohio, and lived in Jerusalem, London, and Philadelphia.

ABOUT THE BOOK

During the Nazi occupation of Holland, the Jewish community suffered devastation on a scale as great as any other nation in Europe. Only a small percentage of Dutch Jews survived the systematic annihilation. The land was flat and easy to patrol, people's backgrounds and religions were well documented, and the physical appearance of most Jews was very distinctive. This is the story of two Jews who did survive and were drawn together by that basic goal of survival. One was an Orthodox Jewish man who, as a member of the Resistance, escaped from the grasp of the Nazis numerous times; fortunately for him, he was never identified as a Jew. The other was a woman whose innocent beauty and very Jewish-looking face compelled her to move from place to place and exhibit unimaginable courage in order to avoid detection and almost certain death at the hands of the Nazis. Together, and with the help of many special people, including a couple whose righteousness reached the highest level one can imagine, they lived to tell their story.

ABOUT NARDUS AND SIPORA

Nardus Groen, born in Rotterdam, Holland, grew up in Amsterdam's Orthodox Jewish neighborhood.

Sipora Catharina Rodrigues-Lopes was born and raised in one of Amsterdam's more secular middle class neighborhoods.

Thrust together during the most horrific of times, they would start a family that today consists of 5 children, 12 grandchildren, and 10 great grandchildren.

Nardus became a Rabbi after the war and would immediately have a pulpit in the city of Apeldoorn. He and Sipora, together with their three sons, would move to Surinam, where he would be the leader of the Jewish community. From there they would move to Cincinnati, Ohio where they would have their only daughter and fourth son. They would later move to Lansdale, Pa; Margate, New Jersey; and Philadelphia, before moving back to Arnhem, Netherlands in 1976. Nardus was appointed the Jewish leader of six provinces and Sipora would work as Directress of the Jewish Old Age home in Arhem. They moved to Florida in their later years where they would enjoy their retirement.

Rabbi Nardus Groen passed away on June 13, 2007 at the age of 87.

Sipora Groen turned 90 on January 1, 2012 and is still healthy and vibrant.

Made in the USA
Middletown, DE
23 July 2019